LETTERS OF
A WOMAN HOMESTEADER

LETTERS OF A
WOMAN HOMESTEADER

by

ELINORE PRUITT STEWART

Introduction by

JESSAMYN WEST

University of Nebraska Press, Lincoln:

1961

MANUFACTURED IN THE UNITED STATES OF AMERICA

The Bison Book edition of LETTERS OF A WOMAN
HOMESTEADER is reproduced from the edition
published in May 1914 by Houghton Mifflin Co.

First Bison Book printing October, 1961

Most recent printing shown by first digit below:

8   9   10

FOREWORD

Jessamyn West

In 1909 Elinore Rupert, a widow with a small daughter, left her work in Denver (she calls herself a "washlady") to become a housekeeper for a Wyoming rancher. She did so because she wanted to homestead a place for herself; and the "Reverend Father," she writes, "thought it a good plan to get a position as a housekeeper for some rancher who would advise me about land and water rights."

The rancher, Clyde Stewart, as the Reverend Father may have foreseen, not only advised her about land and water rights, he advised her to marry him. After six weeks as housekeeper, Elinore Rupert became Elinore Stewart, housewife. "Ranch work seemed to require that we be married first and do our sparking afterward," she wrote Juliet Coney, her former employer. And she continued to write Mrs. Coney during the years that followed. This volume is made up of a selection from those letters.

I first read "The Letters of a Woman Homesteader" in back copies of the *Atlantic Monthly*. I had never forgotten these letters, but on rereading them I found that I had not remembered them as they are. They are, in fact (though not that alone), a collection of short stories. In almost every letter Elinore Stewart

v

tells a story, a true story based on the life of, or some incident in the life of, a neighbor. But what I remembered, and what makes these letters so good are not these stories but the character of the storyteller, of Elinore Stewart herself.

The great letter-writers have not been, in their letters, at least, storytellers: incidents, anecdotes, occasional extended narratives, yes. The great letter-writers have been their own heroes and the deeds they have reported are their own. Elinore Stewart had two reasons, I think, for so often making others the heroes of her letters. First of all, she was a born storyteller with a novelist's eye for those persons and events which have in them the seeds of development, or of irony and reverses, which make good narrative possible. And she had also the born storyteller's need to be heard. She could tell a story, but the telling was pointless without a listener. Secondly, Elinore Stewart was a woman of considerable humility. She wanted her letters to be entertaining, and she supposed that Mrs. Coney might grow tired of hearing only of her. Hence she enlivened her letters with her stories of her neighbors.

Her letters *are* entertaining, but they are so in spite of her stories rather than because of them. We would all, I think, rather know more about Elinore Stewart and less about Zebbie and Gavotte and Cora Belle. And Elinore Stewart's letters endure and give pleasure after fifty years because she does what the great letter-writers do: she reveals herself. True, the nature of the land in which she lives and the work she does, because they are a part of our vanished past, interest us. But it is the woman in this vanished landscape, the homesteader with her enormous vitality, humor and tenderness who holds our attention. We envy her ability to marry in haste and enjoy at leisure. We marvel at her capacity for work. We admire her openness to the world and its inhabitants. Unlike many ranchers, she is a nature-lover, and there are passages in her letters which a Muir or a Burroughs might have written. She always, as she says of her friend Mrs. O'Shaugnessy, "noticed." And what she "noticed," she wrote about to Mrs. Coney. Exposed both to "range talk" and the formal language of the books she read, her letters are neither self-consciously literary nor determinedly colloquial. "Every log in my house is as straight as a pine can grow," she wrote to her friend, and her sentences were built like her house.

We are the beneficiaries of this busy woman's responsiveness to life and of her generous desire to share her experiences. She "proved up" on a good deal more than one hundred and sixty acres and has passed on to us the deed to a possession which time can only enhance, as the reality of the "old West" is progressively obscured by those who portray it most often.

PUBLISHERS' NOTE

THE writer of the following letters is a young woman who lost her husband in a railroad accident and went to Denver to seek support for herself and her two-year-old daughter, Jerrine. Turning her hand to the nearest work, she went out by the day as house-cleaner and laundress. Later, seeking to better herself, she accepted employment as a housekeeper for a well-to-do Scotch cattle-man, Mr. Stewart, who had taken up a quarter-section in Wyoming. The letters, written through several years to a former employer in Denver, tell the story of her new life in the new country. They are genuine letters, and are printed as written, except for occasional omissions and the alteration of some of the names.

May 1914

CONTENTS

CONTENTS

LETTERS OF
A WOMAN HOMESTEADER

LETTERS OF
A WOMAN HOMESTEADER

I

THE ARRIVAL AT BURNT FORK

BURNT FORK, WYOMING,
April 18, 1909.

DEAR MRS. CONEY, —

Are you thinking I am lost, like the Babes in the Wood? Well, I am not and I'm sure the robins would have the time of their lives getting leaves to cover me out here. I am 'way up close to the Forest Reserve of Utah, within half a mile of the line, sixty miles from the railroad. I was twenty-four hours on the train and two days on the stage, and oh, those two days! The snow was just beginning to melt and the mud was about the worst I ever heard of.

The first stage we tackled was just about

as rickety as it could very well be and I had
to sit with the driver, who was a Mormon and
so handsome that I was not a bit offended
when he insisted on making love all the way,
especially after he told me that he was a
widower Mormon. But, of course, as I had
no chaperone I looked very fierce (not that
that was very difficult with the wind and
mud as allies). and told him my actual opinion of Mormons in general and particular.

Meantime my new employer, Mr. Stewart,
sat upon a stack of baggage and was dreadfully concerned about something he calls his
"Tookie," but I am unable to tell you what
that is. The road, being so muddy, was full
of ruts and the stage acted as if it had the
hiccoughs and made us all talk as though we
were affected in the same way. Once Mr.
Stewart asked me if I did not think it a "gey
duir trip." I told him he could call it gay if
he wanted to, but it did n't seem very hila-
rious to me. Every time the stage struck
a rock or a rut Mr. Stewart would "hoot,"

until I began to wish we would come to a hollow tree or a hole in the ground so he could go in with the rest of the owls.

At last we "arriv," and everything is just lovely for me. I have a very, very comfortable situation and Mr. Stewart is absolutely no trouble, for as soon as he has his meals he retires to his room and plays on his bagpipe, only he calls it his "bugpeep." It is "The Campbells are Coming," without variations, at intervals all day long and from seven till eleven at night. Sometimes I wish they would make haste and get here.

There is a saddle horse especially for me and a little shotgun with which I am to kill sage chickens. We are between two trout streams, so you can think of me as being happy when the snow is through melting and the water gets clear. We have the finest flock of Plymouth Rocks and get so many nice eggs. It sure seems fine to have all the cream I want after my town experiences. Jerrine is making good use of all the good things we are having. She rides the pony to water every day.

I have not filed on my land yet because the snow is fifteen feet deep on it, and I think I would rather see what I am getting, so will wait until summer. They have just three seasons here, winter and July and August. We are to plant our garden the last of May. When it is so I can get around I will see about land and find out all I can and tell you.

I think this letter is about to reach thirty-secondly, so I will send you my sincerest love and quit tiring you. Please write me when you have time.

Sincerely yours,

ELINORE RUPERT.

II

May 24, 1909.

DEAR, DEAR MRS. CONEY, —

Well, I have filed on my land and am now a bloated landowner. I waited a long time to even *see* land in the reserve, and the snow is yet too deep, so I thought that as they have but three months of summer and spring together and as I wanted the land for a ranch anyway, perhaps I had better stay in the valley. So I have filed adjoining Mr. Stewart and I am well pleased. I have a grove of twelve swamp pines on my place, and I am going to build my house there. I thought it would be very romantic to live on the peaks amid the whispering pines, but I reckon it would be powerfully uncomfortable also, and I guess my twelve can whisper enough for me; and a dandy thing is, I have all the nice snow-water I want; a small

7

stream runs right through the center of my land and I am quite near wood.

A neighbor and his daughter were going to Green River, the county-seat, and said I might go along, so I did, as I could file there as well as at the land office; and oh, that trip! I had more fun to the square inch than Mark Twain or Samantha Allen *ever* provoked. It took us a whole week to go and come. We camped out, of course, for in the whole sixty miles there was but one house, and going in that direction there is not a tree to be seen, nothing but sage, sand, and sheep. About noon the first day out we came near a sheep-wagon, and stalking along ahead of us was a lanky fellow, a herder, going home for dinner. Suddenly it seemed to me I should starve if I had to wait until we got where we had planned to stop for dinner, so I called out to the man, "Little Bo-Peep, have you anything to eat? If you have, we'd like to find it." And he answered, "As soon as I am able it shall be on the table, if you'll but

trouble to get behind it." Shades of Shake-
speare! Songs of David, the Shepherd Poet!
What do you think of us? Well, we got behind it, and a more delicious "it" I never
tasted. Such coffee! And out of *such* a pot! I
promised Bo-Peep that I would send him a
crook with pink ribbons on it, but I suspect
he thinks I am a crook without the ribbons.

The sagebrush is so short in some places
that it is not large enough to make a fire, so
we had to drive until quite late before we
camped that night. After driving all day
over what seemed a level desert of sand, we
came about sundown to a beautiful cañon,
down which we had to drive for a couple of
miles before we could cross. In the cañon the
shadows had already fallen, but when we
looked up we could see the last shafts of sun-
light on the tops of the great bare buttes.
Suddenly a great wolf started from somewhere and galloped along the edge of the
cañon, outlined black and clear by the set-
ting sun. His curiosity overcame him at last,

so he sat down and waited to see what manner of beast we were. I reckon he was disappointed for he howled most dismally. I thought of Jack London's "The Wolf."

After we quitted the cañon I saw the most beautiful sight. It seemed as if we were driving through a golden haze. The violet shadows were creeping up between the hills, while away back of us the snow-capped peaks were catching the sun's last rays. On every side of us stretched the poor, hopeless desert, the sage, grim and determined to live in spite of starvation, and the great, bare, desolate buttes. The beautiful colors turned to amber and rose, and then to the general tone, dull gray. Then we stopped to camp, and such a scurrying around to gather brush for the fire and to get supper! Everything tasted so good! Jerrine ate like a man. Then we raised the wagon tongue and spread the wagon sheet over it and made a bedroom for us women. We made our beds on the warm, soft sand and went to bed.

FILING A CLAIM

It was too beautiful a night to sleep, so I put my head out to look and to think. I saw the moon come up and hang for a while over the mountain as if it were discouraged with the prospect, and the big white stars flirted shamelessly with the hills. I saw a coyote come trotting along and I felt sorry for him, having to hunt food in so barren a place, but when presently I heard the whirr of wings I felt sorry for the sage chickens he had disturbed. At length a cloud came up and I went to sleep, and next morning was covered several inches with snow. It did n't hurt us a bit, but while I was struggling with stubborn corsets and shoes I communed with myself, after the manner of prodigals, and said: "How much better that I were down in Denver, even at Mrs. Coney's, digging with a skewer into the corners seeking dirt which *might* be there, yea, even eating codfish, than that I should perish on this desert — of imagination." So I turned the current of my imagination and fancied that I was at home before the fireplace, and that the backlog was about to roll down. My fancy was in such good working trim that before I knew it I kicked the wagon wheel, and I certainly got as warm as the most "sot" Scientist that ever read Mrs. Eddy could possibly wish.

After two more such days I "arrived." When I went up to the office where I was to file, the door was open and the most taciturn old man sat before a desk. I hesitated at the door, but he never let on. I coughed, yet no sign but a deeper scowl. I stepped in and modestly kicked over a chair. He whirled around like I had shot him. "Well?" he interrogated. I said, "I am powerful glad of it. I was afraid you were sick, you looked in such pain." He looked at me a minute, then grinned and said he thought I was a book-agent. Fancy me, a fat, comfortable widow, trying to sell books!

Well, I filed and came home. If you will believe me, the Scot was glad to see me and did n't herald the Campbells for two hours after I got home. I'll tell you, it is mighty seldom any one's so much appreciated.

No, we have no rural delivery. It is two miles to the office, but I go whenever I like. It is really the jolliest kind of fun to gallop down. We are sixty miles from the railroad, but when we want anything we send by the mail-carrier for it, only there is nothing to get.

I know this is an inexcusably long letter, but it is snowing so hard and you know how I like to talk. I am sure Jerrine will enjoy the cards and we will be glad to get them. Many things that are a comfort to us out here came from dear Mrs. ——. Baby has the rabbit you gave her last Easter a year ago. In Denver I was afraid my baby would grow up devoid of imagination. Like all the kindergartners, she depended upon others to amuse her. I was very sorry about it, for my castles in Spain have been real homes to me. But there is no fear. She has a block of wood she found in the blacksmith shop which she calls her "dear baby." A spoke out of a wagon wheel is "little Margaret," and a barrel-stave is "bad little Johnny."

Well, I must quit writing before you vote me a nuisance. With lots of love to you,

Your sincere friend,

ELINORE RUPERT.

III

A BUSY, HAPPY SUMMER

September 11, 1909.

DEAR MRS. CONEY, —

This has been for me the busiest, happiest summer I can remember. I have worked very hard, but it has been work that I really enjoy. Help of any kind is very hard to get here, and Mr. Stewart had been too confident of getting men, so that haying caught him with too few men to put up the hay. He had no man to run the mower and he could n't run both the mower and the stacker, so you can fancy what a place he was in.

I don't know that I ever told you, but my parents died within a year of each other and left six of us to shift for ourselves. Our people offered to take one here and there among them until we should all have a place, but we refused to be raised on the halves and so arranged to stay at Grandmother's and keep together. Well, we had no money to hire men to do our work, so had to learn to do it ourselves. Consequently I learned to do many things which girls more fortunately situated don't even know have to be done. Among the things I learned to do was the way to run a mowing-machine. It cost me many bitter tears because I got sunburned, and my hands were hard, rough, and stained with machine oil, and I used to wonder how any Prince Charming could overlook all that in any girl he came to. For all I had ever read of the Prince had to do with his "reverently kissing her lily-white hand," or doing some other fool trick with a hand as white as a snowflake. Well, when my Prince showed up he did n't lose much time in letting me know that "Barkis was willing," and I wrapped my hands in my old checked apron and took him up before he could catch his breath. Then there was no more mowing, and I almost forgot that I knew how until Mr. Stewart got into such a panic. If he put a man to mow, it kept them all idle at the stacker, and he just could n't get enough men. I was afraid to tell him I could mow for fear he would forbid me to do so. But one morning, when he was chasing a last hope of help, I went down to the barn, took out the horses, and went to mowing. I had enough cut before he got back to show him I knew how, and as he came back manless he was delighted as well as surprised. I was glad because I really like to mow, and besides that, I am adding feathers to my cap in a surprising way. When you see me again you will think I am wearing a feather duster, but it is only that I have been said to have almost as much sense as a "mon," and that is an honor I never aspired to, even in my wildest dreams.

I have done most of my cooking at night, have milked seven cows every day, and have done all the hay-cutting, so you see I have been working. But I have found time to put up thirty pints of jelly and the same amount of jam for myself. I used wild fruits, goose-berries, currants, raspberries, and cherries. I have almost two gallons of the cherry butter, and I think it is delicious. I wish I could get some of it to you, I am sure you would like it.

We began haying July 5 and finished September 8. After working so hard and so steadily I decided on a day off, so yesterday I saddled the pony, took a few things I needed, and Jerrine and I fared forth. Baby can ride behind quite well. We got away by sunup and a glorious day we had. We followed a stream higher up into the mountains and the air was so keen and clear at first we had on our coats. There was a tang of sage and of pine in the air, and our horse was midside deep in rabbit-brush, a shrub just covered with flowers that look and smell like goldenrod. The blue distance promised many alluring adventures, so we went along singing and simply gulping in summer. Occasionally a bunch of sage chickens would fly up out of the sagebrush, or a jack rabbit

would leap out. Once we saw a bunch of
antelope gallop over a hill, but we were out
just to be out, and game did n't tempt us. I
started, though, to have just as good a time as
possible, so I had a fish-hook in my knapsack.

Presently, about noon, we came to a little
dell where the grass was as soft and as green
as a lawn. The creek kept right up against
the hills on one side and there were groves
of quaking asp and cottonwoods that made
shade, and service-bushes and birches that
shut off the ugly hills on the other side. We
dismounted and prepared to noon. We
caught a few grasshoppers and I cut a birch
pole for a rod. The trout are so beautiful now,
their sides are so silvery, with dashes of old
rose and orange, their speckles are so black,
while their backs look as if they had been
sprinkled with gold-dust. They bite so well
that it does n't require any especial skill or
tackle to catch plenty for a meal in a few
minutes.

In a little while I went back to where I had

left my pony browsing, with eight beauties. We made a fire first, then I dressed my trout while it was burning down to a nice bed of coals. I had brought a frying-pan and a bottle of lard, salt, and buttered bread. We gathered a few service-berries, our trout were soon browned, and with water, clear, and as cold as ice, we had a feast. The quaking aspens are beginning to turn yellow, but no leaves have fallen. Their shadows dimpled and twinkled over the grass like happy children. The sound of the dashing, roaring water kept inviting me to cast for trout, but I did n't want to carry them so far, so we rested until the sun was getting low and then started for home, with the song of the locusts in our ears warning us that the melancholy days are almost here. We would come up over the top of a hill into the glory of a beautiful sunset with its gorgeous colors, then down into the little valley already purpling with mysterious twilight. So on, until, just at dark, we rode into our corral and a

A BUSY, HAPPY SUMMER

mighty tired, sleepy little girl was powerfully glad to get home.

After I had mailed my other letter I was afraid that you would think me plumb bold about the little Bo-Peep, and was a heap sorrier than you can think. If you only knew the hardships these poor men endure. They go two together and sometimes it is months before they see another soul, and rarely ever a woman. I would n't act so free in town, but these men see people so seldom that they are awkward and embarrassed. I like to put them at ease, and it is to be done only by being kind of hail-fellow-well-met with them. So far not one has ever misunderstood me and I have been treated with every courtesy and kindness, so I am powerfully glad you understand. They really enjoy doing these little things like fixing our dinner, and if my poor company can add to any one's pleasure I am too glad.

Sincerely yours,
ELINORE RUPERT.

A WOMAN HOMESTEADER

Mr. Stewart is going to put up my house for me in pay for my extra work.

I am ashamed of my long letters to you, but I am such a murderer of language that I have to use it all to tell anything.

Please don't entirely forget me. Your letters mean so much to me and I will try to answer more promptly.

IV

A CHARMING ADVENTURE AND ZEBULON PIKE

September 28, 1909.

DEAR MRS. CONEY, —

Your second card just reached me and I am plumb glad because, although I answered your other, I was wishing I could write you, for I have had the most charming adventure.

It is the custom here for as many women as care to to go in a party over into Utah to Ashland (which is over a hundred miles away) after fruit. They usually go in September, and it takes a week to make the trip. They take wagons and camp out and of course have a good time, but, the greater part of the way, there is n't even the semblance of a road and it is merely a semblance anywhere. They came over to invite me to join them. I was of two minds — I wanted to go, but it seemed a little risky and a big chance for discomfort,

23

since we would have to cross the Uinta Mountains, and a snowstorm likely any time. But I did n't like to refuse outright, so we left it to Mr. Stewart. His "Ye're nae gang" sounded powerful final, so the ladies departed in awed silence and I assumed a martyr-like air and acted like a very much abused woman, although he did only what I wanted him to do. At last, in sheer desperation he told me the "bairn canna stand the treep," and that was why he was so determined. I knew why, of course, but I continued to look abused lest he gets it into his head that he can boss me. After he had been reduced to the proper plane of humility and had explained and begged my pardon and had told me to consult only my own pleasure about going and coming and using his horses, only not to "expoose" the bairn, why, I forgave him and we were friends once more.

Next day all the men left for the round-up, to be gone a week. I knew I never could stand myself a whole week. In a little while the ladies came past on their way to Ashland. They were all laughing and were so happy that I really began to wish I was one of the number, but they went their way and I kept wanting to go *somewhere*. I got reckless and determined to do something real bad. So I went down to the barn and saddled Robin Adair, placed a pack on "Jeems McGregor," then Jerrine and I left for a camping-out expedition.

It was nine o'clock when we started and we rode hard until about four, when I turned Robin loose, saddle and all, for I knew he would go home and some one would see him and put him into the pasture. We had gotten to where we could n't ride anyway, so I put Jerrine on the pack and led "Jeems" for about two hours longer; then, as I had come to a good place to camp, we stopped.

While we had at least two good hours of daylight, it gets so cold here in the evening that fire is very necessary. We had been climbing higher into the mountains all day and had reached a level tableland where the grass was luxuriant and there was plenty of wood and water. I unpacked "Jeems" and staked him out, built a roaring fire, and made our bed in an angle of a sheer wall of rock where we would be protected against the wind. Then I put some potatoes into the embers, as Baby and I are both fond of roasted potatoes. I started to a little spring to get water for my coffee when I saw a couple of jack rabbits playing, so I went back for my little shotgun. I shot one of the rabbits, so I felt very like Leather-stocking because I had killed but one when I might have gotten two. It was fat and young, and it was but the work of a moment to dress it and hang it up on a tree. Then I fried some slices of bacon, made myself a cup of coffee, and Jerrine and I sat on the ground and ate. Everything smelled and tasted so good! This air is so tonic that one gets delightfully hungry. Afterward we watered and restaked "Jeems," I rolled some logs on to the fire, and then we sat and enjoyed the prospect.

The moon was so new that its light was very dim, but the stars were bright. Presently a long, quivering wail arose and was answered from a dozen hills. It seemed just the sound one ought to hear in such a place. When the howls ceased for a moment we could hear the subdued roar of the creek and the crooning of the wind in the pines. So we rather enjoyed the coyote chorus and were not afraid, because they don't attack people. Presently we crept under our Navajos and, being tired, were soon asleep.

I was awakened by a pebble striking my cheek. Something prowling on the bluff above us had dislodged it and it struck me. By my Waterbury it was four o'clock, so I arose and spitted my rabbit. The logs had left a big bed of coals, but some ends were still burning and had burned in such a manner that the heat would go both under and over my rabbit. So I put plenty of bacon grease over him and hung him up to roast. Then I went back to bed. I did n't want to start early because the air is too keen for comfort early in the morning.

The sun was just gilding the hilltops when we arose. Everything, even the barrenness, was beautiful. We have had frosts, and the quaking aspens were a trembling field of gold as far up the stream as we could see. We were 'way up above them and could look far across the valley. We could see the silvery gold of the willows, the russet and bronze of the currants, and patches of cheerful green showed where the pines were. The splendor was relieved by a background of sober gray-green hills, but even on them gay streaks and patches of yellow showed where rabbit-brush grew. We washed our faces at the spring, — the grasses that grew around the edge and dipped into the water were loaded with ice, — our rabbit was done to a turn, so I made some delicious coffee, Jerrine got herself a can of water, and we breakfasted.

A CHARMING ADVENTURE

Shortly afterwards we started again. We did n't know where we were going, but we were on our way.

That day was more toilsome than the last, but a very happy one. The meadowlarks kept singing like they were glad to see us. But we were still climbing and soon got beyond the larks and sage chickens and up into the timber, where there are lots of grouse. We stopped to noon by a little lake, where I got two small squirrels and a string of trout. We had some trout for dinner and salted the rest with the squirrels in an empty can for future use. I was anxious to get a grouse and kept close watch, but was never quick enough. Our progress was now slower and more difficult, because in places we could scarcely get through the forest. Fallen trees were everywhere and we had to avoid the branches, which was powerful hard to do. Besides, it was quite dusky among the trees long before night, but it was all so grand and awe-inspiring. Occasionally there was an opening through which we could see the snowy peaks, seemingly just beyond us, toward which we were headed. But when you get among such grandeur you get to feel how little you are and how foolish is human endeavor, except that which reunites us with the mighty force called God. I was plumb uncomfortable, because all my own efforts have always been just to make the best of everything and to take things as they come.

At last we came to an open side of the mountain where the trees were scattered. We were facing south and east, and the mountain we were on sheered away in a dangerous slant. Beyond us still greater wooded mountains blocked the way, and in the cañon between night had already fallen. I began to get scary. I could only think of bears and catamounts, so, as it was five o'clock, we decided to camp. The trees were immense. The lower branches came clear to the ground and grew so dense that any tree afforded a splendid shelter from the weather, but I was nervous and wanted one that would protect us against any possible attack. At last we found one growing in a crevice of what seemed to be a sheer wall of rock. Nothing could reach us on two sides, and in front two large trees had fallen so that I could make a log heap which would give us warmth and make us safe. So with rising spirits I unpacked and prepared for the night. I soon had a roaring fire up against the logs and, cutting away a few branches, let the heat into as snug a bedroom as any one could wish. The pine needles made as soft a carpet as the wealthiest could afford. Springs abound in the mountains, so water was plenty. I staked "Jeems" quite near so that the firelight would frighten away any wild thing that tried to harm him. Grass was very plentiful, so when he was made "comfy" I made our bed and fried our trout. The branches had torn off the bag in which I had my bread, so it was lost in the forest, but who needs bread when they have good, mealy potatoes? In a short time we were eating like Lent was just over. We lost all the glory of the sunset except what we got by reflection, being on the side of the mountain we were, with the dense woods between. Big sullen clouds kept drifting over and a wind got lost in the trees that kept them rocking and groaning in a horrid way. But we were just as cozy as we could be and rest was as good as anything.

I wish you could once sleep on the kind of bed we enjoyed that night. It was both soft and firm, with the clean, spicy smell of the pine. The heat from our big fire came in and we were warm as toast. It was so good to stretch out and rest. I kept thinking how superior I was since I dared to take such an outing when so many poor women down in Denver were bent on making their twenty cents per hour in order that they could spare a quarter to go to the "show." I went to sleep with a powerfully self-satisfied feeling, but I awoke to realize that pride goeth before a fall.

A CHARMING ADVENTURE

I could hardly remember where I was when I awoke, and I could almost hear the silence. Not a tree moaned, not a branch seemed to stir. I arose and my head came in violent contact with a snag that was not there when I went to bed. I thought either I must have grown taller or the tree shorter during the night. As soon as I peered out, the mystery was explained.

Such a snowstorm I never saw! The snow had pressed the branches down lower, hence my bumped head. Our fire was burning merrily and the heat kept the snow from in front. I scrambled out and poked up the fire; then, as it was only five o'clock, I went back to bed. And then I began to think how many kinds of idiot I was. Here I was thirty or forty miles from home, in the mountains where no one goes in the winter and where I knew the snow got to be ten or fifteen feet deep. But I could never see the good of moping, so I got up and got breakfast while Baby put her shoes on. We had our squirrels and more baked potatoes and I had delicious black coffee.

After I had eaten I felt more hopeful. I knew Mr. Stewart would hunt for me if he knew I was lost. It was true, he would n't know which way to start, but I determined to rig up "Jeems" and turn him loose, for I knew he would go home and that he would leave a trail so that I could be found. I hated to do so, for I knew I should always have to be powerfully humble afterwards. Anyway it was still snowing, great, heavy flakes; they looked as large as dollars. I did n't want to start "Jeems" until the snow stopped because I wanted him to leave a clear trail. I had sixteen loads for my gun and I reasoned that I could likely kill enough food to last twice that many days by being careful what I shot at. It just kept snowing, so at last I decided to take a little hunt and provide for the day. I left Jerrine happy with the towel rolled into a baby, and went along the brow of the mountain for almost a mile, but the snow fell so thickly that I could n't see far. Then I happened to look down into the cañon that lay east of us and saw smoke. I looked toward it a long time, but could make out nothing but smoke, but presently I heard a dog bark and I knew I was near a camp of some kind. I resolved to join them, so went back to break my own camp.

At last everything was ready and Jerrine and I both mounted. Of all the times! If you think there is much comfort, or even security, in riding a pack-horse in a snow-storm over mountains where there is no road, you are plumb wrong. Every once in a while a tree would unload its snow down our backs. "Jeems" kept stumbling and threatening to break our necks. At last we got down the mountain-side, where new danger confronted us, — we might lose sight of the smoke or ride into a bog. But at last, after what seemed hours, we came into a "clearing" with a small log house and, what is rare in

A WOMAN HOMESTEADER

Wyoming, a fireplace. Three or four hounds set up their deep baying, and I knew by the chimney and the hounds that it was the home of a Southerner. A little old man came bustling out, chewing his tobacco so fast, and almost frantic about his suspenders, which it seemed he could n't get adjusted.

As I rode up, he said, "Whither, friend?" I said "Hither." Then he asked, "Air you spying around for one of them dinged game wardens arter that deer I killed yisteddy?" I told him I had never even seen a game warden and that I did n't know he had killed a deer. "Wall," he said, "air you spying around arter that gold mine I diskivered over on the west side of Baldy?" But after a while I convinced him that I was no more nor less than a foolish woman lost in the snow. Then he said, "Light, stranger, and look at your saddle." So I "lit" and looked, and then I asked him what part of the South he was from. He answered, "Yell County, by gum! The best place in the United States, or in the world, either." That was my introduction to Zebulon Pike Parker.

Only two "Johnny Rebs" could have enjoyed each other's company as Zebulon Pike and myself did. He was so small and so old, but so cheerful and so sprightly, and a real Southerner! He had a big, open fireplace with backlogs and andirons. How I enjoyed it all! How we feasted on some of the deer killed "yisteddy," and real corn-pone baked in a skillet down on the hearth. He was so full of happy recollections and had a few that were not so happy! He is, in some way, a kinsman of Pike of Pike's Peak fame, and he came west "jist arter the wah" on some expedition and "jist stayed." He told me about his home life back in Yell County, and I feel that I know all the "young uns."

There was George Henry, his only brother; and there were Phœbe and "Mothie," whose real name is Martha; and poor little Mary Ann, whose death was described so feelingly that no one could keep back the tears. Lastly there was little Mandy, the baby and his favorite, but who, I am afraid, was a selfish little beast since she had to have her prunellas when all the rest of the "young uns" had to wear shoes that old Uncle Buck made out of rawhide. But then "her eyes were blue as morning-glories and her hair was jist like corn-silk, so yaller and fluffy." Bless his simple, honest heart! His own eyes are blue and kind, and his poor, thin little shoulders are so round that they almost meet in front. How he loved to talk of his boyhood days! I can almost see his father and George Henry as they marched away to the "wah" together, and the poor little mother's despair as she waited day after day for some word, that never came.

Poor little Mary Ann was drowned in the bayou, where she was trying to get water-lilies. She had wanted a white dress all her life and so, when she was dead, they took down the white cross-bar curtains and

A CHARMING ADVENTURE

Mother made the little shroud by the light of a tallow dip. But, being made by hand, it took all the next day, too, so that they buried her by moonlight down back of the orchard under the big elm where the children had always had their swing. And they lined and covered her grave with big, fragrant water-lilies. As they lowered the poor little home-made coffin into the grave the mockingbirds began to sing and they sang all that dewy, moonlight night. Then little Mandy's wedding to Judge Carter's son Jim was described. She wore a "cream-colored poplin with a red rose throwed up in it," and the lace that was on Grandma's wedding dress. There were bowers of sweet Southern roses and honeysuckle and wistaria. Don't you know she was a dainty bride?

At last it came out that he had not heard from home since he left it. "Don't you ever write?" I asked. "No, I am not an eddicated man, although I started to school.

A WOMAN HOMESTEADER

Yes'm, I started along of the rest, but they
told me it was a Yankee teacher and I was
'fraid, so when I got most to the schoolhouse
I hid in the bushes with my spelling-book, so
that is all the learning I ever got. But my
mother was an eddicated woman, yes'm, she
could both read and write. I have the Bible
she give me yit. Yes'm, you jist wait and
I'll show you." After some rummaging in
a box he came back with a small leather-
bound Bible with print so small it was hard
to read. After turning to the record of births
and deaths he handed it to me, his wrinkled
old face shining with pride as he said, "There,
my mother wrote that with her own hand."
I took the book and after a little deciphered
that "Zebulon Pike Parker was born Feb.
10, 1830," written in the stiff, difficult style
of long ago and written with pokeberry ink.
He said his mother used to read about some
"old feller that was jist covered with biles,"
so I read Job to him, and he was full of surprise they did n't "git some cherry bark and

some sasparilly and bile it good and gin it to him."

He had a side room to his cabin, which was his bedroom; so that night he spread down a buffalo robe and two bearskins before the fire for Jerrine and me. After making sure there were no moths in them, I spread blankets over them and put a sleepy, happy little girl to bed, for he had insisted on making molasses candy for her because they happened to be born on the same day of the month. And then he played the fiddle until almost one o'clock. He played all the simple, sweet, old-time pieces, in rather a squeaky, jerky way, I am afraid, but the music suited the time and the place.

Next morning he called me early and when I went out I saw such a beautiful sunrise, well worth the effort of coming to see. I had thought his cabin in a cañon, but the snow had deceived me, for a few steps from the door the mountains seemed to drop down suddenly for several hundred feet and the first of the snow peaks seemed to lie right at our feet. Around its base is a great swamp, in which the swamp pines grow very thickly and from which a vapor was rising that got about halfway up the snow peak all around. Fancy to yourself a big jewel-box of dark green velvet lined with silver chiffon, the snow peak lying like an immense opal in its center and over all the amber light of a new day. That is what it looked most like.

Well, we next went to the corral, where I was surprised to find about thirty head of sheep. Some of them looked like they should have been sold ten years before. "Don't you ever sell any of your sheep?" I asked. "No'm. There was a feller come here once and wanted to buy some of my wethers, but I would n't sell any because I did n't need any money." Then he went from animal to animal, caressing each and talking to them, calling them each by name. He milked his one cow, fed his two little mules, and then we went back to the house to cook breakfast.

A CHARMING ADVENTURE

We had delicious venison steak, smoking hot, and hoe-cakes and the "bestest" coffee, and honey.

After breakfast we set out for home. Our pack transferred to one of the little mules, we rode "Jeems," and Mr. Parker rode the other mule. He took us another way, down cañon after cañon, so that we were able to ride all the time and could make better speed. We came down out of the snow and camped within twelve miles of home in an old, deserted ranch house. We had grouse and sage chicken for supper. I was so anxious to get home that I could hardly sleep, but at last I did and was only awakened by the odor of coffee, and barely had time to wash before Zebulon Pike called breakfast. Afterwards we fixed "Jeems's" pack so that I could still ride, for Zebulon Pike was very anxious to get back to his "critters."

Poor, lonely, childlike little man! He tried to tell me how glad he had been to entertain me. "Why," he said, "I was plumb glad to see you and right sorry to have you go. Why, I would jist as soon talk to you as to a nigger. Yes'm, I would. It has been almost as good as talking to old Aunt Dilsey." If a Yankee had said the same to me I would have demanded instant apology, but I know how the Southern heart longs for the dear, kindly old "niggers," so I came on homeward, thankful for the first time that I can't talk correctly.

I got home at twelve and found, to my joy, that none of the men had returned, so I am safe from their superiority for a while, at least.

With many apologies for this outrageous letter, I am

Your ex-Washlady,
ELINORE RUPERT.

V

November 22, 1909.

My dear Friend, —

I was dreadfully afraid that my last letter was too much for you and now I feel plumb guilty. I really don't know how to write you, for I have to write so much to say so little, and now that my last letter made you sick I almost wish so many things did n't happen to me, for I always want to tell you. Many things have happened since I last wrote, and Zebulon Pike is not done for by any means, but I guess I will tell you my newest experience.

I am making a wedding dress. Don't grin; it is n't mine, — worse luck! But I must begin at the beginning. Just after I wrote you before, there came a terrific storm which made me appreciate indoor coziness, but as

45

only Baby and I were at home I expected to be very lonely. The snow was just whirling when I saw some one pass the window. I opened the door and in came the dumpiest little woman and two daughters. She asked me if I was "Mis' Rupit." I told her that she had almost guessed it, and then she introduced herself. She said she was "Mis' Lane," that she had heard there was a new stranger in the country, so she had brought her twin girls, Sedalia and Regalia, to be neighborly. While they were taking off their many coats and wraps it came out that they were from Linwood, thirty miles away. I was powerful glad I had a pot roast and some baked beans.

After we had put the horses in the barn we had dinner and I heard the story of the girls' odd names. The mother is one of those "comfy," fat little women who remain happy and bubbling with fun in spite of hard knocks. I had already fallen in love with Regalia, she is so jolly and unaffected, so fat and so plain.

SEDALIA AND REGALIA

Sedalia has a veneer of most uncomfortable refinement. She was shocked because Gale ate all the roast she wanted, and if I had been very sensitive I would have been in tears, because I ate a helping more than Gale did.

But about the names. It seemed that "Mis' Lane" married quite young, was an orphan, and had no one to tell her things she should have known. She lived in Missouri, but about a year after her marriage the young couple started overland for the West. It was in November, and one night when they had reached the plains a real blue blizzard struck them. "Mis' Lane" had been in pain all day and soon she knew what was the matter. They were alone and it was a day's travel back to the last house. The team had given out and the wind and sleet were seeing which could do the most meanness. At last the poor man got a fire started and a wagon sheet stretched in such a manner that it kept off the sleet. He fixed a bed under the poor shelter and did all he could to keep the fire from blowing away, and there, a few hours later, a little girl baby was born. They melted sleet in the frying-pan to get water to wash it. "Mis' Lane" kept feeling no better fast, and about the time they got the poor baby dressed a second little one came.

That she told me herself is proof she did n't die, I guess, but it is right hard to believe she did n't. Luckily the fire lasted until the babies were dressed and the mother began to feel better, for there was no wood. Soon the wind stopped and the snow fell steadily. It was warmer, and the whole family snuggled up under the wagon sheet and slept.

Mr. Lane is a powerful good husband. He waited two whole days for his wife to gain strength before he resumed the journey, and on the third morning he actually carried her to the wagon. Just think of it! Could more be asked of any man?

Every turn of the wheels made poor "Mis' Lane" more homesick. Like Mrs. Wiggs of the Cabbage Patch, she had a taste for geographical names, and "Mis' Lane" is very loyal, so she wanted to call the little first-born "Missouri." Mr. Lane said she might, but that if she did he would call the other one "Arkansas." Sometimes homesickness would almost master her. She would hug up the little red baby and murmur "Missouri," and then daddy would growl playfully to "Arkansas." It went on that way for a long time and at last she remembered that Sedalia was in Missouri, so she felt glad and really named the older baby "Sedalia." But she could think of nothing to match the name and was in constant fear the father would name the other baby "Little Rock."

For three years poor Gale was just "t'other one." Then the Lanes went to Green River where some lodge was having a parade. They were watching the drill when a "bystander that was standing by" said something about the "fine regalia." Instantly "Mis' Lane" thought of her unnamed child; so since that time Gale has had a name.

There could be no two people more unlike than the sisters. Sedalia is really handsome, and she is thin. But she is vain, selfish, shallow, and conceited. Gale is not even pretty, but she is clean and she is honest. She does many little things that are not exactly polite, but she is good and true. They both went to the barn with me to milk. Gale tucked up her skirts and helped me. She said, "I just love a stable, with its hay and comfortable, contented cattle. I never go into one without thinking of the little baby Christ. I almost expect to see a little red baby in the straw every time I peek into a manger."

Sedalia answered, "Well, for Heaven's sake, get out of the stable to preach. Who wants to stand among these smelly cows all day?"

They stayed with us almost a week, and one day when Gale and I were milking she asked me to invite her to stay with me a month. She said to ask her mother, and left her mother and myself much together. But Sedalia stuck to her mother like a plaster and I just could not stand Sedalia a whole month. However, I was spared all embarrassment, for "Mis' Lane" asked me if I could not find work enough to keep Gale busy for a month or two. She went on to explain that Sedalia was expecting to be married and that Gale was so "common" she would really spoil the match. I was surprised and indignant, especially as Sedalia sat and listened so brazenly, so I said I thought Sedalia would need all the help she could get to get married and that I should be glad to have Gale visit me as long as she liked.

So Gale stayed on with me. One afternoon she had gone to the post-office when I saw Mr. Patterson ride up. He went into the bunk-house to wait until the men should come. Now, from something Gale had said I fancied that Bob Patterson must be the right man. I am afraid I am not very delicate

about that kind of meddling, and while I had
been given to understand that Patterson was
the man Sedalia expected to marry, I did n't
think any man would choose her if he could
get Gale, so I called him. We had a long
chat and he told me frankly he wanted Gale,
but that she did n't care for him, and that
they kept throwing "that danged Sedalia"
at him. Then he begged my pardon for saying "danged," but I told him I approved of
the word when applied to Sedalia, and broke
the news to him that Gale was staying with
me. He fairly beamed. So that night I left
Gale to wash dishes and Bob to help her
while I held Mr. Stewart a prisoner in the
stable and questioned him regarding Patterson's prospects and habits. I found both all
that need be, and told Mr. Stewart about my
talk with Patterson, and he said, "Wooman,
some day ye 'll gang ploom daft." But he
admitted he was glad it was the "bonny
lassie, instead of the bony one." When we
went to the house Mr. Stewart said, "Weel,

when are you douchy bairns gangin' to the kirk?"

They left it to me, so I set Thanksgiving Day, and as there is no "kirk to gang to," we are going to have a justice of the peace and they are to be married here. We are going to have the dandiest dinner that I can cook, and Mr. Stewart went to town next day for the wedding dress, the gayest plaid outside of Caledonia. But Gale has lots of sense and is going to wear it. I have it almost finished, and while it does n't look just like a Worth model, still it looks plumb good for me to have made. The boys are going up after Zebulon Pike, and Mr. Stewart is going after "Mis' Lane." Joy waves are radiating from this ranch and about Thanksgiving morning one will strike you.

With lots of love and happy wishes,

Your ex-Washlady,

ELINORE RUPERT.

VI

A THANKSGIVING-DAY WEDDING

DEAR MRS. CONEY, —

. . . I think every one enjoyed our Thanksgiving programme except poor Gale. She was grieved, I verily believe, because Mr. Patterson is not Mormon and could not take Sedalia and herself also. I suppose it seemed odd to her to be unable to give way to Sedalia as she had always done.

I had cooked and cooked. Gale and Zebulon Pike both helped all they could. The wedding was to be at twelve o'clock, so at ten I hustled Gale into my room to dress. I had to lock the door to keep her in, and I divided my time between the last touches to my dinner and the finishing touches to Gale's toilet and receiving the people. The Lane party had not come yet, and I was scared to death lest Sedalia had had a tantrum and

54

that Mr. Stewart would not get back in time. At last I left the people to take care of themselves, for I had too much on my mind to bother with them. Just after eleven Mr. Stewart, Mis' Lane, Sedalia, and Pa Lane "arriv" and came at once into the kitchen to warm. In a little while poor, frightened Gale came creeping in, looking guilty. But she looked lovely, too, in spite of her plaid dress. She wore her hair in a coronet braid, which added dignity and height, as well as being simple and becoming. Her mother brought her a wreath for her hair, of lilies of the valley and tiny pink rosebuds. It might seem a little out of place to one who did n't see it, but the effect was really charming.

Sedalia did n't know that Mr. Stewart had given Gale her dress, so, just to be nasty, she said, as soon as she saw Gale, "Dear me, when are you going to dress, Gale? You will hardly have time to get out of that horse-blanket you are wearing and get into something decent." You see, she thought it was one of my dresses fixed over for Gale. Presently Sedalia asked me if I was invited to the "function." She had some kind of rash on her face and Zebulon Pike noticed the rash and heard the word "function," so he thought that was the name of some disease and asked Mr. Stewart if the "function" was "catching." Mr. Stewart had heard Sedalia, but knew "Zebbie" had not heard all that was said and how he got the idea he had, so he answered, "Yes, if ye once get the fever." So Zebulon Pike privately warned every one against getting the "function" from Sedalia. There are plenty of people here who don't know exactly what a function is, myself among them. So people edged away from Sedalia, and some asked her if she had seen the doctor and what he thought of her case. Poor girl, I'm afraid she did n't have a very enjoyable time.

At last the "jestice" of the peace came, and I hope they live happy ever afterward.

THANKSGIVING–DAY WEDDING

That night a dance was given to celebrate the event and we began to have dinner immediately after the wedding so as to get through in time to start, for dances are never given in the home here, but in "the hall." Every settlement has one and the invitations are merely written announcements posted everywhere. We have what Sedalia calls "homogenous" crowds. I would n't attempt to say what she means, but as everybody goes no doubt she is right.

Our dinner was a success, but that is not to be wondered at. Every woman for miles around contributed. Of course we had to borrow dishes, but we could n't think of seating every one; so we set one table for twenty-four and had three other long tables, on one of which we placed all the meats, pickles, and sauces, on another the vegetables, soup, and coffee, and on the third the pie, cakes, ice-cream, and other desserts. We had two big, long shelves, one above the other, on which were the dishes. The people helped themselves to dishes and neighbors took turns at serving from the tables, so people got what they wanted and hunted themselves a place to sit while they ate. Two of the cowboys from this ranch waited upon the table at which were the wedding party and some of their friends. Boys from other ranches helped serve and carried coffee, cake, and ice-cream. The tablecloths were tolerably good linen and we had ironed them wet so they looked nice. We had white lace-paper on the shelves and we used drawn-work paper napkins. As I said, we borrowed dishes, or, that is, every woman who called herself our neighbor brought whatever she thought we would need. So after every one had eaten I suggested that they sort out their dishes and wash them, and in that way I was saved all that work. We had everything done and were off to the dance by five o'clock. We went in sleds and sleighs, the snow was so deep, but it was all so jolly. Zebbie, Mr. Stewart, Jerrine, and I went in the bobsled.

THANKSGIVING–DAY WEDDING

We jogged along at a comfortable pace lest the "beasties" should suffer, and every now and then a merry party would fly past us scattering snow in our faces and yelling like Comanches. We had a lovely moon then and the snow was so beautiful! We were driving northward, and to the south and back of us were the great somber, pine-clad Uintah Mountains, while ahead and on every side were the bare buttes, looking like old men of the mountains, — so old they had lost all their hair, beard, and teeth.

VII

December 28, 1909.

DEAR MRS. CONEY, — Our Thanksgiving affair was the most enjoyable happening I can remember for a long time. Zebulon Pike came, but I had as a bait for him two fat letters from home. As soon as I came back from his place I wrote to Mrs. Carter and trusted to luck for my letter to reach her. I told her all I could about her brother and how seldom he left his mountain home. I asked her to write him all she could in one letter, as the trips between our place and his were so few and far between. So when she received my letter she wrote all she could think of, and then sent her letter and mine to Mothie and Phœbe, who are widows living in the old home. They each took turns writing, so their letters are a complete record of the years "Zebbie" has been gone. The letters were addressed to me along with a cordial letter from Mrs. Carter asking me to see that he got them and to use my judgment in the delivering. I could n't go myself, but I wanted to read the letters to him and to write the answers; so I selected one piece of news I felt would bring him to hear the rest without his knowing how much there was for him.

Well, the boys brought him, and a more delighted little man I am sure never lived. I read the letters over and over, and answers were hurried off. He was dreadfully homesick, but could n't figure on how he could leave the "critters," or how he could trust himself on a train. Mr. Stewart became interested, and he is a very resourceful man, so an old Frenchman was found who had no home and wanted a place to stay so he could trap. He was installed at Zebulon Pike's with full instructions as to each "critter's" peculiarities and needs. Then one of the boys, who was going home for Christmas to Memphis, was induced to wait for Mr. Parker and to see him safe to Little Rock. His money was banked for him, and Mr. Stewart saw that he was properly clothed and made comfortable for the trip. Then he sent a telegram to Judge Carter, who met Zebulon Pike at Little Rock, and they had a family reunion in Yell County. I have had some charming letters from there, but that only proves what I have always said, that I am the luckiest woman in finding really lovely people and having really happy experiences. Good things are constantly happening to me. I wish I could tell you about my happy Christmas, but one of my New Year's resolutions was to stop loading you down with two-thousand-word letters.

From something you wrote I think I must have written boastingly to you at some time. I have certainly not intended to, and you must please forgive me and remember how ignorant I am and how hard it is for me to express myself properly. I felt after I had written to Mr. Parker's people that I had taken a liberty, but luckily it was not thought of in that way by them. If you only knew how far short I fall of my own hopes you would know I could *never* boast. Why, it keeps me busy making over mistakes just like some one using old clothes. I get myself all ready to enjoy a success and find that I have to fit a failure. But one consolation is that I generally have plenty of material to cut generously, and many of my failures have proved to be real blessings.

I do hope this New Year may bring to you the desire of your heart and all that those who love you best most wish for you.

With lots and lots of love from baby and myself.

Your ex-washlady,

ELINORE STEWART.

VIII

A HAPPY CHRISTMAS

DEAR MRS. CONEY, —

My happy Christmas resulted from the ex-sheriff of this county being snowbound here. It seems that persons who come from a lower altitude to this country frequently become bewildered, especially if in poor health, leave the train at any stop and wander off into the hills, sometimes dying before they are found. The ex-sheriff cited a case, that of a young German who was returning from the Philippines, where he had been discharged after the war. He was the only child of his widowed mother, who has a ranch a few miles from here. No one knew he was coming home. One day the cook belonging to the camp of a construction gang went hunting and came back running, wild with horror. He had found the body of a man. The coro-

64

ner and the sheriff were notified, and next morning went out for the body, but the wolves had almost destroyed it. High up in a willow, under which the poor man had lain down to die, they saw a small bundle tied in a red bandanna and fast to a branch. They found a letter addressed to whoever should find it, saying that the body was that of Benny Louderer and giving them directions how to spare his poor old mother the awful knowledge of how he died. Also there was a letter to his mother asking her not to grieve for him and to keep their days faithfully. "Their days," I afterward learned, were anniversaries which they had always kept, to which was added "Benny's day."

Poor boy! When he realized that death was near his every thought was for the mother. Well, they followed his wishes, and the casket containing the bare, gnawed bones was sealed and never opened. And to this day poor Mrs. Louderer thinks her boy died of some fever while yet aboard the transport.

A WOMAN HOMESTEADER

The manner of his death has been kept so secret that I am the only one who has heard it.

I was so sorry for the poor mother that I resolved to visit her the first opportunity I had. I am at liberty to go where I please when there is no one to cook for. So, when the men left, a few days later, I took Jerrine and rode over to the Louderer ranch. I had never seen Mrs. Louderer and it happened to be "Benny's day" that I blundered in upon. I found her to be a dear old German woman living all alone, the people who do the work on the ranch living in another house two miles away. She had been weeping for hours when I got there, but in accordance with her custom on the many anniversaries, she had a real feast prepared, although no one had been bidden.

She says that God always sends her guests, but that was the first time she had had a little girl. She had a little daughter once herself, little Gretchen, but all that was left was a sweet memory and a pitifully small mound on the ranch, quite near the house, where Benny and Gretchen are at rest beside "der fader, Herr Louderer."

She is such a dear old lady! She made us so welcome and she is so entertaining. All the remainder of the day we listened to stories of her children, looked at her pictures, and Jerrine had a lovely time with a wonderful wooden doll that they had brought with them from Germany. Mrs. Louderer forgot to weep in recalling her childhood days and showing us her treasures. And then our feast, — for it was verily a feast. We had goose and it was *so* delicious. I could n't tell you half the good things any more than I could have eaten some of all of them.

We sat talking until far into the night, and she asked me how I was going to spend Christmas. I told her, "Probably in being homesick." She said that would never do and suggested that we spend it together. She said it was one of their special days and that the only happiness left her was in mak-

ing some one else happy; so she had thought
of cooking some nice things and going to as
many sheep camps as she could, taking with
her the good things to the poor exiles, the
sheep-herders. I liked the plan and was glad
to agree, but I never dreamed I should have
so lovely a time. When the queer old wooden
clock announced two we went to bed.

I left quite early the next morning with
my head full of Christmas plans. You may
not know, but cattle-men and sheep-men
cordially hate each other. Mr. Stewart is
a cattle-man, and so I did n't mention my
Christmas plans to him. I saved all the
butter I could spare for the sheep-herders;
they never have any. That and some jars of
gooseberry jelly was all I could give them.
I cooked plenty for the people here, and two
days before Christmas I had a chance to go
down to Mrs. Louderer's in a buggy, so we
went. We found her up to her ears in cooking, and such sights and smells I could never
describe. She was so glad I came early, for

she needed help. I never worked so hard in my life or had a pleasanter time.

Mrs. Louderer had sent a man out several days before to find out how many camps there were and where they were located. There were twelve camps and that means twenty-four men. We roasted six geese, boiled three small hams and three hens. We had besides several meat-loaves and links of sausage. We had twelve large loaves of the *best* rye bread; a small tub of doughnuts; twelve coffee-cakes, more to be called fruit-cakes, and also a quantity of little cakes with seeds, nuts, and fruit in them, — so pretty to look at and *so* good to taste. These had a thick coat of icing, some brown, some pink, some white. I had thirteen pounds of butter and six pint jars of jelly, so we melted the jelly and poured it into twelve glasses.

The plan was, to start real early Christmas Eve morning, make our circuit of camps, and wind up the day at Frau O'Shaughnessy's to spend the night. Yes, Mrs. O'Shaughnessy

A WOMAN HOMESTEADER

is Irish, — as Irish as the pigs in Dublin.
Before it was day the man came to feed and
to get our horses ready. We were up betimes
and had breakfast. The last speck was wiped
from the shining stove, the kitchen floor was
scrubbed, and the last small thing put in
order. The man had four horses harnessed
and hitched to the sled, on which was placed
a wagon-box filled with straw, hot rocks,
and blankets. Our twelve apostles — that
is what we called our twelve boxes — were
lifted in and tied firmly into place. Then
we clambered in and away we went. Mrs.
Louderer drove, and Tam O'Shanter and
Paul Revere were snails compared to us.
We did n't follow any road either, but went
sweeping along across country. No one else
in the world could have done it unless they
were drunk. We went careening along hill-
sides without even slacking the trot. Occasionally we struck a particularly stubborn
bunch of sagebrush and even the sled-runners
would jump up into the air. We did n't stop

to light, but hit the earth several feet in advance of where we left it. Luck was with us, though. I hardly expected to get through with my head unbroken, but not even a glass was cracked.

It would have done your heart good to see the sheep-men. They were all delighted, and when you consider that they live solely on canned corn and tomatoes, beans, salt pork, and coffee, you can fancy what they thought of their treat. They have mutton when it is fit to eat, but that is certainly not in winter. One man at each camp does the cooking and the other herds. It does n't make any difference if the cook never cooked before, and most of them never did. At one camp, where we stopped for dinner, they had a most interesting collection of fossils. After delivering our last "apostle," we turned our faces toward Frau O'Shaughnessy's, and got there just in time for supper.

Mrs. O'Shaughnessy is a widow, too, and has quite an interesting story. She is a dumpy little woman whose small nose seems to be smelling the stars, it is so tip-tilted. She has the merriest blue eyes and the quickest wit. It is really worth a severe bumping just to be welcomed by her. It was so warm and cozy in her low little cabin. She had her table set for supper, but she laid plates for us and put before us a beautifully roasted chicken. Thrifty Mrs. Louderer thought it should have been saved until next day, so she said to Frau O'Shaughnessy, "We hate to eat your hen, best you save her till tomorrow." But Mrs. O'Shaughnessy answered, "Oh, 't is no mather, 't is an ould hin she was annyway." So we enjoyed the "ould hin," which was brown, juicy, and tender.

When we had finished supper and were drinking our "tay," Mrs. O'Shaughnessy told our fortunes with the tea-leaves. She told mine first and said I would die an old maid. I said it was rather late for that, but she cheerfully replied, "Oh, well, better late than

A HAPPY CHRISTMAS

niver." She predicted for Mrs. Louderer that she should shortly catch a beau. "'T is the next man you see that will come coortin' you." Before we left the table some one knocked and a young man, a sheep-herder, entered. He belonged to a camp a few miles away and is out from Boston in search of health. He had been into town and his horse was lamed so he could not make it into camp, and he wanted to stay overnight. He was a stranger to us all, but Mrs. O'Shaughnessy made him at home and fixed such a tempting supper for him that I am sure he was glad of the chance to stay. He was very decidedly English, and powerfully proud of it. He asked Mrs. O'Shaughnessy if she was Irish and she said, "No, ye haythen, it's Chinese Oi am. Can't yez tell it be me Cockney accint?" Mr. Boutwell looked very much surprised. I don't know which was the funnier, the way he looked or what she said.

We had a late breakfast Christmas morning, but before we were through Mr. Stewart came. We had planned to spend the day with Mrs. O'Shaughnessy, but he did n't approve of our going into the sheep district, so when he found where we had gone he came after us. Mrs. Louderer and he are old acquaintances and he bosses her around like he tries to boss me. Before we left, Mrs. O'Shaughnessy's married daughter came, so we knew she would not be lonely.

It was almost one o'clock when we got home, but all hands helped and I had plenty cooked anyway, so we soon had a good dinner on the table. Mr. Stewart had prepared a Christmas box for Jerrine and me. He does n't approve of white waists in the winter. I had worn one at the wedding and he felt personally aggrieved. For me in the box were two dresses, that is, the material to make them. One is a brown and red checked, and the other green with a white fleck in, both outing flannel. For Jerrine there was a pair of shoes and stockings, both stockings full of candy and nuts. He is very bluff in manner, but he is really the kindest person.

Mrs. Louderer stayed until New Year's day. My Christmas was really a very happy one.

Your friend,

ELINORE RUPERT.

. . . An interesting day on this ranch is the day the cattle are named. If Mr. Stewart had children he would as soon think of leaving them unnamed as to let a "beastie" go without a name.

On the day they vaccinated he came into the kitchen and told me he would need me to help him name the "critters." So he and I "assembled" in a safe place and took turns naming the calves. As fast as a calf was vaccinated it was run out of the chute and he or I called out a name for it and it was booked that way.

The first two he named were the "Duke of Monmouth" and the "Duke of Montrose." I called my first "Oliver Cromwell" and "John Fox." The poor "mon" had to have revenge, so the next ugly, scrawny little beast he called the "Poop of Roome." And it was a heifer calf, too.

This morning I had the startling news that the "Poop" had eaten too much alfalfa and was all "swellit oop," and, moreover, he had "stealit it." I don't know which is the more astonishing, that the Pope has stolen alfalfa, or that he has eaten it.

We have a swell lot of names, but I am not sure I could tell you which is "Bloody Mary," or which is "Elizabeth," or, indeed, which is which of any of them.

E. R.

IX

A CONFESSION

April 5, 1910.

DEAR MRS. CONEY, —

I find upon re-reading your letter that I did not answer it at all when I wrote you. You must think me very indifferent, but I really don't mean to be.

My house joins on to Mr. Stewart's house. It was built that way so that I could "hold down" my land and job at the same time. I see the wisdom of it now, though at first I did not want it that way. My boundary lines run within two feet of Mr. Stewart's house, so it was quite easy to build on.

I think the Pattersons' ranch is about twenty-five miles from us. I am glad to tell you they are doing splendidly. Gale is just as thrifty as she can be and Bobby is steady and making money fast. Their baby is the dearest little thing. I have heard that Sedalia is to marry a Mormon bishop, but I doubt it. She puts on very disgusting airs about "our Bobby," and she patronizes Gale most shamefully; but Gale, bless her unconscious heart, is so happy in her husband and son that she does n't know Sedalia is insulting.

My dear old grandmother whom I loved so much has gone home to God. I used to write long letters to her. I should like a few addresses of old persons who are lonely as she was, who would like letters such as I write. You know I can't be brief. I have tried and cannot. If you know of any persons who would not tire of my long accounts and would care to have them, you will be doing me a favor to let me know.

I have not treated you quite frankly about something you had a right to know about. I am ashamed and I regret very much that I have not told you. I so dread the possibility of losing your friendship that I will *never* tell

A CONFESSION

you unless you promise me beforehand to forgive me. I know that is unfair, but it is the only way I can see out of a difficulty that my foolish reticence has led me into. Few people, perhaps, consider me reticent, but in some cases I am afraid I am even deceitful. Won't you make it easy to "'fess" so I may be happy again?

Truly your friend,

ELINORE RUPERT.

June 16, 1910.

MY DEAR FRIEND, —

Your card just to hand. I wrote you some time ago telling you I had a confession to make and have had no letter since, so thought perhaps you were scared I had done something too bad to forgive. I am suffering just now from eye-strain and can't see to write long at a time, but I reckon I had better confess and get it done with.

The thing I have done is to marry Mr. Stewart. It was such an inconsistent thing to do that I was ashamed to tell you. And, too, I was afraid you would think I did n't need your friendship and might desert me. Another of my friends thinks that way.

I hope my eyes will be better soon and then I will write you a long letter.

Your old friend with a new name,

ELINORE STEWART.

X

THE STORY OF CORA BELLE

August 15, 1910.

DEAR MRS. CONEY, —

. . . Grandma Edmonson's birthday is the 30th of May, and Mrs. O'Shaughnessy suggested that we give her a party. I had never seen Grandma, but because of something that happened in her family years ago which a few narrow-heads whom it did n't concern in the least cannot forgive or forget, I had heard much of her. The family consists of Grandma, Grandpa, and little Cora Belle, who is the sweetest little bud that ever bloomed upon the twigs of folly.

The Edmonsons had only one child, a daughter, who was to have married a man whom her parents objected to solely because he was a sheep-man, while their sympathies were with the cattle-men, although they owned only a small bunch. To gain their consent the young man closed out his interest in sheep, at a loss, filed on a splendid piece of land near them, and built a little home for the girl he loved. Before they could get to town to be married Grandpa was stricken with rheumatism. Grandma was already almost past going on with it, so they postponed the marriage, and as that winter was particularly severe, the young man took charge of the Edmonson stock and kept them from starving. As soon as he was able he went for the license.

Mrs. O'Shaughnessy and a neighbor were hunting some cattle that had wandered away and found the poor fellow shot in the back. He was not yet dead and told them it was urgently necessary for them to hurry him to the Edmonsons' and to get some one to perform the marriage ceremony as quickly as possible, for he could not live long. They told him such haste meant quicker death because he would bleed more; but he insisted, so they got a wagon and hurried all they could. But they could not outrun death. When he knew he could not live to reach home, he asked them to witness all he said. Everything he possessed he left to the girl he was to have married, and said he was the father of the little child that was to come. He begged them to befriend the poor girl he had to leave in such a condition, and to take the marriage license as evidence that he had tried to do right. The wagon was stopped so the jolting would not make death any harder, and there in the shadow of the great twin buttes he died.

They took the body to the little home he had made, and Mrs. O'Shaughnessy went to the Edmonsons' to do what she could there. Poor Cora Jane did n't know how terrible a thing wounded pride is. She told her parents her misdeeds. They could n't see that they were in any way to blame. They seemed to care nothing for her terrible sorrow nor for her weakened condition. All they could think of was that the child they had almost worshiped had disgraced them; so they told her to go.

Mrs. O'Shaughnessy took her to the home that had been prepared for her, where the poor body lay. Some way they got through those dark days, and then began the waiting for the little one to come. Poor Cora Jane said she would die then, and that she wanted to die, but she wanted the baby to know it was loved, — she wanted to leave something that should speak of that love when the child should come to understanding. So Mrs. O'Shaughnessy said they would make all its little clothes with every care, and they should tell of the love. Mrs. O'Shaughnessy is the daintiest needleworker I have ever seen; she was taught by the nuns at St. Catherine's in the "ould country." She was all patience with poor, unskilled Cora Jane, and the little outfit that was finally finished was dainty enough for a fairy. Little Cora Belle is so proud of it.

THE STORY OF CORA BELLE

At last the time came and Mrs. O'Shaughnessy went after the parents. Long before, they had repented and were only too glad to go. The poor mother lived one day and night after the baby came. She laid the tiny thing in her mother's arms and told them to call her Cora Belle. She told them she gave them a pure little daughter in place of the sinful one they had lost.

That was almost twelve years ago, and the Edmonsons have lived in the new house all this time. The deed to the place was made out to Cora Belle, and her grandfather is her guardian. . . .

If you traveled due north from my home, after about nine hours' ride you would come into an open space in the butte lands, and away between two buttes you would see the glimmer of blue water. As you drew nearer you would be able to see the fringe of willows around the lake, and presently a low, red-roofed house with corrals and stables. You would see long lines of "buck" fence, a flock of sheep near by, and cattle scattered about feeding. This is Cora Belle's home. On the long, low porch you would see two old folks rocking. The man is small, and has rheumatism in his legs and feet so badly that he can barely hobble. The old lady is large and fat, and is also afflicted with rheumatism, but has it in her arms and shoulders. They are both cheerful and hopeful, and you would get a cordial welcome. . . .

When you saw Cora Belle you would see a stout, square-built little figure with long flaxen braids, a pair of beautiful brown eyes and the longest and whitest lashes you ever saw, a straight nose, a short upper lip, a broad, full forehead, — the whole face, neither pretty nor ugly, plentifully sown with the brownest freckles. She is very truly the head of the family, doing all the housework and looking after the stock, winter and summer, entirely by herself. Three years ago she took things into her own hands, and since that time has managed altogether. Mrs.

THE STORY OF CORA BELLE

O'Shaughnessy, however, tells her what to do.

The sheep, forty in number, are the result of her individual efforts. Mrs. O'Shaughnessy told her there was more money in raising lambs than in raising chickens, so she quit the chickens as a business and went to some of the big sheep-men and got permission to take the "dogie" lambs, which they are glad to give away. She had plenty of cows, so she milked cows and fed lambs all day long all last year. This year she has forty head of nice sheep worth four dollars each, and she does n't have to feed them the year round as she would chickens, and the wolves are no worse to kill sheep than they are to kill chickens. When shearing-time came she went to a sheep-man and told him she would help cook for his men one week if he would have her sheep sheared with his. She said her work was worth three dollars, that is what one man would get a day shearing, and he could easily shear her sheep in one day.

A WOMAN HOMESTEADER

That is how she got her sheep sheared. The man had her wool hauled to town with his, sold it for her, and it brought sixty dollars. She took her money to Mrs. O'Shaughnessy. She wanted some supplies ordered before she went home, because, as she gravely said, "the rheumatiz would get all the money she had left when she got home," — meaning that her grandparents would spend what remained for medicine.

The poor old grandparents read all the time of wonderful cures that different dopes accomplish, and they spend every nickel they can get their hands on for nostrums. They try everything they read of, and have to buy it by the case, — horrid patent stuff! They have rolls of testimonials and believe every word, so they keep on trying and hoping. When there is any money they each order whatever medicine they want to try. If Mrs. Edmonson's does n't seem to help her, Grandpa takes it and she takes his, — that is their idea of economy. They would spend hours telling you about their different remedies and would offer you spoonful after spoonful of vile-looking liquid, and be mildly grieved when you refused to take it. Grandma's hands are so bent and twisted that she can't sew, so dear old Grandpa tries to do it.

Mrs. O'Shaughnessy told me that she helped out when she could. Three years ago she made them all a complete outfit, but the "rheumatiz" has been getting all the spare money since then, so there has been nothing to sew. A peddler sold them a piece of gingham which they made up for Cora Belle. It was broad pink and white stripes, and they wanted some style to "Cory's" clothes, so they cut a gored skirt. But they had no pattern and made the gores by folding a width of the goods biasly and cutting it that way. It was put together with no regard to matching the stripes, and a bias seam came in the center behind, but they put no stay in the seam and the result was the most outrageous affair imaginable.

A WOMAN HOMESTEADER

Well, we had a large room almost empty and Mr. Stewart liked the idea of a party, so Mrs. Louderer, Mrs. O'Shaughnessy, and myself planned for the event. It was to be a sewing-bee, a few good neighbors invited, and all to sew for Grandma. . . . So Mrs. O'Shaughnessy went to Grandma's and got all the material she had to make up. I had saved some sugar-bags and some flour-bags. I knew Cora Belle needed underwear, so I made her some little petticoats of the larger bags and some drawers of the smaller. I had a small piece of white lawn that I had no use for, and of that I made a dear little sunbonnet with a narrow edging of lace around, and also made a gingham bonnet for her. Two days before the time, came Mrs. Louderer, laden with bundles, and Mrs. O'Shaughnessy, also laden. We had all been thinking of Cora Belle. Mr. Stewart had sent by mail for her a pair of sandals for everyday wear and a nice pair of shoes, also some stockings. Mrs. Louderer brought cloth for three dresses of heavy Dutch calico, and gingham for three aprons. She made them herself and she sews so carefully. She had bought patterns and the little dresses were stylishly made, as well as well made. Mrs. O'Shaughnessy brought a piece of crossbar with a tiny forget-me-not polka dot, and also had goods and embroidery for a suit of underwear. My own poor efforts were already completed when the rest came, so I was free to help them.

Late in the afternoon of the 29th a funny something showed up. Fancy a squeaky, rickety old wagon without a vestige of paint. The tires had come off and had been "set" at home; that is done by heating the tires red-hot and having the rims of the wheels covered with several layers of burlap, or other old rags, well wet; then the red-hot tire is put on and water hurriedly poured on to shrink the iron and to keep the burlap from blazing. Well, whoever had set Cora Belle's tires had forgotten to cut away the surplus burlap, so all the ragtags were merrily waving in the breeze.

Cora Belle's team would bring a smile to the soberest face alive. Sheba is a tall, lanky old mare. Once she was bay in color, but the years have added gray hair until now she is roan. Being so long-legged she strides along at an amazing pace which her mate, Balaam, a little donkey, finds it hard to keep up with. Balaam, like Sheba, is full of years. Once his glossy brown coat was the pride of some Mexican's heart, but time has added to his color also, and now he is blue. His eyes are sunken and dim, his ears no longer stand up in true donkey style, but droop dejectedly. He has to trot his best to keep up with Sheba's slowest stride. About every three miles he balks, but little Cora Belle does n't call it balking, she says Balaam has stopped to rest, and they sit and wait till he is ready to trot along again. That is the kind of layout which drew up before our door that evening. Cora Belle was driving and she wore her

THE STORY OF CORA BELLE

wonderful pink dress which hung down in a peak behind, fully six inches longer than anywhere else. The poor child had no shoes. The winter had tried the last pair to their utmost endurance and the "rheumatiz" had long since got the last dollar, so she came with her chubby little sunburned legs bare. Her poor little scarred feet were clean, her toe-nails full of nicks almost into the quick, broken against rocks when she had been herding her sheep. In the back of the wagon, flat on the bottom, sat Grandma and Grandpa, such bundles of coats and blankets I can't describe. After a great deal of trouble we got them unloaded and into the house. Then Mrs. Louderer entertained them while Mrs. O'Shaughnessy and I prepared supper and got a bath ready for Cora Belle. We had a T-bone steak, mashed potatoes, hominy, hot biscuits and butter, and stewed prunes. Their long ride had made them hungry and I know they enjoyed their meal.

After supper Cora Belle and I washed the

dishes while Mrs. O'Shaughnessy laid out the little clothes. Cora Belle's clothes were to be a surprise. The postmistress here also keeps a small store and has ribbon, and when she heard of our plans from Mr. Stewart she sent up a couple of pairs of hair-ribbon for Cora Belle. Soon Mrs. O'Shaughnessy called us, and Cora Belle and I went into the bedroom where she was. I wish you could have seen that child! Poor little neglected thing, she began to cry. She said, "They ain't for me, I know they ain't. Why, it ain't my birthday, it's Granny's." Nevertheless, she had her arms full of them and was clutching them so tightly with her work-worn little hands that we could n't get them. She sobbed so deeply that Grandma heard her and became alarmed. She hobbled to the door and pounded with her poor twisted hands, calling all the while, "Cory, Cory Belle, what ails you?" She got so excited that I opened the door, but Cora Belle told her to go away. She said, "They ain't for you, Granny, and they ain't for me either." . . .

People here observe Decoration Day faithfully, and Cora Belle had brought half a wagon-load of iris, which grows wild here. Next morning we were all up early, but Cora Belle's flowers had wilted and she had to gather more, but we all hurried and helped. She said as she was going to see her mother she wanted to wear her prettiest dress, so Gale and Mrs. O'Shaughnessy helped her to get ready. The cemetery is only about two miles away, so we were all down quite early. We were obliged to hurry because others were coming to help sew. Cora Belle went at once to the graves where her parents lie side by side, and began talking to her mother just as though she saw her. "You did n't know me, did you, Mother, with my pretty new things? But I am your little girl, Mamma. I am your little Cora Belle." After she had talked and had turned every way like a proud little bird, she went to work.

A WOMAN HOMESTEADER

And, oh, how fast she worked! Both graves were first completely covered with pine boughs. It looked like sod, so closely were the little twigs laid. Next she broke the stems off the iris and scattered the blossoms over, and the effect was very beautiful. Then we hurried home and everybody got busy. The men took Grandpa off to another part of the ranch where they were fanning oats to plant, and kept him all day. That was good for him because then he could be with the men all day and he so seldom has a chance to be with men. Several ladies came and they all made themselves at home and worked like beavers, and we all had a fine time. . . .

Sedalia was present and almost caused a riot. She says she likes unusual words because they lend distinction to conversation. Well, they do — sometimes. There was another lady present whose children are very gifted musically, but who have the bad name of taking what they want without asking. The mother can neither read nor write, and she is very sensitive about the bad name her children have. While we were all busy some one made a remark about how smart these children were. Sedalia thought that a good time to get in a big word, so she said, "Yes, I have always said Lula was a progeny." Mrs. Hall did n't know what she meant and thought that she was casting reflections on her child's honesty, so with her face scarlet and her eyes blazing she said, "Sedalia Lane, I won't allow you nor nobody else to say my child is a progeny. You can take that back or I will slap you peaked." Sedalia took it back in a hurry, so I guess little Lula Hall is not a progeny.

Every one left about four except Gale, Mrs. O'Shaughnessy, Mrs. Louderer, and the Edmonsons. They had farthest to go, so they stayed over night again. We worked until ten o'clock that night over Grandma's clothes, but everything was thoroughly finished. Every button was on, every thread-end knotted and clipped, and some tired workers lay down to rest, as did a very happy child and a very thankful old lady.

Every one got away by ten o'clock the next morning. The last I saw of little Cora Belle was when they had reached the top of a long slope and Balaam had "stopped to rest." The breeze from the south was playfully fluttering the rags on the wheels. Presently I heard a long "hee-haw, hee-haw," and I knew Balaam had rested and had started.

I have been a very busy woman since I began this letter to you several days ago. A dear little child has joined the angels. I dressed him and helped to make his casket. There is no minister in this whole country and I could not bear the little broken lily-bud to be just carted away and buried, so I arranged the funeral and conducted the services. I know I am unworthy and in no way fitted for such a mission, but I did my poor best, and if no one else is comforted, I am. I know the message of God's love and care has been told once, anyway, to people who have learned to believe more strongly in hell than in heaven.

Dear friend, I do hope that this New Year will bring you and yours fuller joys than you have ever known. If I had all the good gifts in my hands you should certainly be blessed.

Your sincere friend,

ELINORE RUPERT STEWART.

XI

ZEBBIE'S STORY

September 1, 1910.

DEAR MRS. CONEY, —

It was just a few days after the birthday party and Mrs. O'Shaughnessy was with me again. We were down at the barn looking at some new pigs, when we heard the big corral gates swing shut, so we hastened out to see who it could be so late in the day.

It was Zebbie. He had come on the stage to Burnt Fork and the driver had brought him on here. . . . There was so much to tell, and he whispered he had something to tell me privately, but that he was too tired then; so after supper I hustled him off to bed. . . .

Next morning . . . the men went off to their work and Zebbie and I were left to tell secrets. When he was sure we were alone he took from his trunk a long, flat box. Inside was the most wonderful shirt I have ever seen; it looked like a cross between a nightshirt and a shirt-waist. It was of homespun linen. The bosom was ruffled and tucked, all done by hand, — such tiny stitches, such patience and skill. Then he handed me an old daguerreotype. I unfastened the little golden hook and inside was a face good to see and to remember. It was dim, yet clear in outline, just as if she were looking out from the mellow twilight of long ago. The sweet, elusive smile, — I could n't tell where it was, whether it was the mouth or the beautiful eyes that were smiling. All that was visible of her dress was the Dutch collar, just like what is being worn now. It was pinned with an ugly old brooch which Zebbie said was a "breast-pin" he had given her. Under the glass on the other side was a strand of faded hair and a slip of paper. The writing on the paper was so faded it was scarcely readable, but it said: "Pauline Gorley, age 22, 1860."

A WOMAN HOMESTEADER

Next he showed me a note written by Pauline, simply worded, but it held a world of meaning for Zebbie. It said, "I spun and wove this cloth at Adeline's, enough for me a dress and you a shirt, which I made. It is for the wedding, else to be buried in. Yours, Pauline." The shirt, the picture, and the note had waited for him all these years in Mothie's care. And now I will tell you the story.

Long, long ago some one did something to some one else and started a feud. Unfortunately the Gorleys were on one side and the Parkers on the other. That it all happened before either Zebbie or Pauline was born made no difference. A Gorley must hate a Parker always, as also a Parker must hate a Gorley. Pauline was the only girl, and she had a regiment of big brothers who gloried in the warfare and wanted only the slightest pretext to shoot a Parker. So they grew up, and Zebbie often met Pauline at the quiltings and other gatherings at the homes of non-partisans. He remembers her so perfectly and describes her so plainly that I can picture her easily. She had brown eyes and hair. She used to ride about on her sorrel palfrey with her "nigger" boy Cæsar on behind to open and shut plantation gates. She wore a pink calico sunbonnet, and Zebbie says "she was just like the pink hollyhocks that grew by mother's window." Is n't that a sweet picture?

Her mother and father were both dead, and she and her brothers lived on their plantation. Zebbie had never dared speak to her until one day he had driven over with his mother and sisters to a dinner given on a neighboring plantation. He was standing outside near the wall, when some one dropped a spray of apple blossoms down upon him from an upper window. He looked up and Pauline was leaning out smiling at him. After that he made it a point to frequent places where he might expect her, and things went so well that presently Cæsar was left at home lest he should tell the brothers. She was a loyal little soul and would not desert, although he urged her to, even promising to go away, "plumb away, clean to Scott County if she would go." She told him that her brothers would go even as far as that to kill him, so that they must wait and hope. Finally Zebbie got tired of waiting, and one day he boldly rode up to the Gorley home and formally asked for Pauline's hand. The bullet he got for his presumption kept him from going to the war with his father and brother when they marched away.

Some time later George Gorley was shot and killed from ambush, and although Zebbie had not yet left his bed the Gorleys believed he did it, and one night Pauline came through a heavy rainstorm, with only Cæsar, to warn Zebbie and to beg him, for her sake, to get away as fast as he could that night. She pleaded that she could not live if he were killed and could never marry him if he killed her brothers, so she persuaded him to go while they were all innocent.

ZEBBIE'S STORY

Well, he did as she wished and they never saw each other again. He never went home again until last Thanksgiving, and dear little Pauline had been dead for years. She herself had taken her little gifts for Zebbie to Mothie to keep for him. Some years later she died and was buried in the dress she mentioned. It was woven at Adeline Carter's, one of the bitterest enemies of the Gorleys, but the sacrifice of her pride did her no good because she was long at rest before Zebbie knew. He had been greatly grieved because no stone marked her grave, only a tangle of rose-briers. So he bought a stone, and in the night before Decoration Day he and two of Uncle Buck's grandsons went to the Gorley burying-ground and raised it to the memory of sweet Pauline. Some of the Gorleys still live there, so he came home at once, fearing if they should find out who placed the stone above their sister they would take vengeance on his poor, frail body.

After he had finished telling me his story,

A WOMAN HOMESTEADER

I felt just as I used to when Grandmother opened the "big chist" to air her wedding clothes and the dress each of her babies wore when baptized. It seemed almost like smelling the lavender and rose-leaves, and it was with reverent fingers that I folded the shirt, the work of love, yellow with age, and laid it in the box. . . .

Well, Mrs. O'Shaughnessy returned, and early one morning we started with a wagon and a bulging mess-box for Zebbie's home. We were going a new and longer route in order to take the wagon. Dandelions spread a carpet of gold. Larkspur grew waist-high with its long spikes of blue. The service-bushes and the wild cherries were a mass of white beauty. Meadowlarks and robins and bluebirds twittered and sang from every branch, it almost seemed. A sky of tenderest blue bent over us and fleecy little clouds drifted lazily across. . . . Soon we came to the pineries, where we traveled up deep gorges and cañons. The sun shot arrows of gold through the pines down upon us and we gathered our arms full of columbines. The little black squirrels barked and chattered saucily as we passed along, and we were all children together. We forgot all about feuds and partings, death and hard times. All we remembered was that God is good and the world is wide and beautiful. We plodded along all day. Next morning there was a blue haze that Zebbie said meant there would be a high wind, so we hurried to reach his home that evening.

The sun was hanging like a great red ball in the smoky haze when we entered the long cañon in which is Zebbie's cabin. Already it was dusky in the cañons below, but not a breath of air stirred. A more delighted man than Zebbie I never saw when we finally drove up to his low, comfortable cabin. Smoke was slowly rising from the chimney, and Gavotte, the man in charge, rushed out and the hounds set up a joyful barking. Gavotte is a Frenchman, and he was all smiles and gesticulations as he said, "Welcome, welcome! To-day I am rejoice you have come. Yesterday I am despair if you have come because I am scrub, but to-day, behold, I am delight."

I have heard of clean people, but Gavotte is the cleanest man I ever saw. The cabin floor was so white I hated to step upon it. The windows shone, and at each there was a calico curtain, blue-and-white check, un-ironed but newly washed. In one window was an old brown pitcher, cracked and nicked, filled with thistles. I never thought them pretty before, but the pearly pink and the silvery green were so pretty and looked so clean that they had a new beauty. Above the fireplace was a great black eagle which Gavotte had killed, the wings outspread and a bunch of arrows in the claws. In one corner near the fire was a washstand, and behind it hung the fishing-tackle. Above one door was a gun-rack, on which lay the rifle and shotgun, and over the other door was a pair of deer-antlers. In the center of the room stood the square home-made table, every inch scrubbed. In the side room, which is the bedroom, was a wide bunk made of pine plank that had also been scrubbed, then filled with fresh, sweet pine boughs, and over them was spread a piece of canvas that had once been a wagon sheet, but Gavotte had washed it and boiled and pounded it until it was clean and sweet. That served for a sheet.

Zebbie was beside himself with joy. The hounds sprang upon him and expressed their joy unmistakably. He went at once to the corrals to see the "critters," and every one of them was safely penned for the night. "Old Sime," an old ram (goodness knows *how* old!), promptly butted him over, but he just beamed with pleasure. "Sime knows me, dinged if he don't!" was his happy exclamation. We went into the cabin and left him fondling the "critters."

Gavotte did himself proud getting supper. We had trout and the most delicious biscuit.

A WOMAN HOMESTEADER

Each of us had a crisp, tender head of lettuce with a spoonful of potato salad in the center. We had preserves made from canned peaches, and the firmest yellow butter. Soon it was quite dark and we had a tiny brass lamp which gave but a feeble light, but it was quite cool so we had a blazing fire which made it light enough.

When supper was over, Zebbie called us out and asked us if we could hear anything. We could hear the most peculiar, long-drawn, sighing wail that steadily grew louder and nearer. I was really frightened, but he said it was the forerunner of the windstorm that would soon strike us. He said it was wind coming down Crag Cañon, and in just a few minutes it struck us like a cold wave and rushed, sighing, on down the cañon. We could hear it after it had passed us, and it was perfectly still around the cabin. Soon we heard the deep roaring of the coming storm, and Zebbie called the hounds in and secured the door. The sparks began to fly up the chimney. Jerrine lay on a bearskin before the fire, and Mrs. O'Shaughnessy and I sat on the old blue "settle" at one side. Gavotte lay on the other side of the fire on the floor, his hands under his head. Zebbie got out his beloved old fiddle, tuned up, and began playing. Outside the storm was raging, growing worse all the time. Zebbie played and played. The worse the tumult, the harder the storm, the harder he played. I remember I was holding my breath, expecting the house to be blown away every moment, and Zebbie was playing what he called "Bonaparte's Retreat." It all seemed to flash before me — I could see those poor, suffering soldiers staggering along in the snow, sacrifices to one man's unholy ambition. I verily believe we were all bewitched. I should n't have been surprised to have seen witches and gnomes come tumbling down the chimney or flying in at the door, riding on the crest of the storm. I glanced at Mrs. O'Shaughnessy. She sat with her chin in her hand, gazing with unseeing eyes into the fire. Zebbie seemed possessed; he could n't tire.

It seemed like hours had passed and the tumult had not diminished. I felt like shriek-ing, but I gathered Jerrine up into my arms and carried her in to bed. Mrs. O'Shaugh-nessy came with us. She touched my elbow and said, "Child, don't look toward the win-dow, the banshees are out to-night." We knelt together beside the bed and said our beads; then, without undressing save pulling off our shoes, we crawled under our blankets and lay on the sweet, clean pine. We were both perfectly worn out, but we could not sleep. There seemed to be hundreds of dif-ferent noises of the storm, for there are so many cañons, so many crooks and turns, and the great forest too. The wind was shrieking, howling, and roaring all at once. A deep boom announced the fall of some giant of the forest. I finally dozed off even in that terrible din, but Zebbie was not so frenzied as he had been. He was playing "Annie Laurie," and that song has always been a favorite of mine. The storm began gradually to die away and "Annie Laurie" sounded so beautiful. I was thinking of Pauline and, I know, to Zebbie, Annie Laurie and Pauline Gorley are one and the same.

I knew no more until I heard Zebbie call out, "Ho, you sleepy-heads, it's day." Mrs. O'Shaughnessy turned over and said she was still sleepy. My former visit had taught me what beauty the early morning would spread before me, so I dressed hastily and went out-doors. Zebbie called me to go for a little walk. The amber light of the new day was chasing the violet and amethyst shadows down the cañons. It was all more beautiful than I can tell you. On one side the cañon-walls were almost straight up. It looked as if we might step off into a very world of mountains. Soon Old Baldy wore a crown of gleaming gold. The sun was up. We walked on and soon came to a brook. We were washing our faces in its icy waters when we heard twigs breaking, so we stood perfectly still. From out the undergrowth of birch and willows came a deer with two fawns. They stopped to drink, and nibbled the bushes. But soon they scented strangers, and, looking about with their beautiful, startled eyes, they saw us and away they went like the wind. We saw many great trees uptorn by the storm. High up on the cliffs Zebbie showed me where the eagles built every year. . . . We turned homeward and sat down upon the trunk of a fallen pine to rest and take another look at the magnificent view. Zebbie was silent, but presently he threw a handful of pebbles down the cañon wall. "I am not sorry Pauline is dead. I have never shed a tear. I know you think that is odd, but I have never wanted to mourn. I am glad that it is as it is. I am happy and at peace because I know she is mine. The little breeze is Pauline's own voice; she had a little caressing way just like the gentlest breeze when it stirs your hair. There is something in everything that brings back Pauline: the beauty of the morning, the song of a bird or the flash of its wings. The flowers look like she did. So I have not lost her, she is mine more than ever. I have always felt so, but was never quite sure until I went back and saw where they laid her. I know people think I am crazy, but I don't care for that. I shall not hate to die. When you get to be as old as I am, child, everything will have a new meaning to you."

At last we slowly walked back to the cabin, and at breakfast Zebbie told of the damage the storm had done. He was so commonplace that no one ever would have guessed his strange fancy. . . .

I shall never forget Zebbie as I last saw him. It was the morning we started home. After we left the bench that Zebbie lives on, our road wound down into a deeper cañon. Zebbie had followed us to where a turn in the cañon should hide us from view. I looked back and saw him standing on the cliffs, high above us, the early morning sun turning his snowy hair to gold, the breeze-fingers of Pauline tossing the scanty locks. I shall always remember him so, a living monument to a dead past.

ELINORE STEWART.

XII

A CONTENTED COUPLE

October 6, 1911.

DEAR MRS. CONEY, —

. . . I once "heared" Sedalia Lane telling some of her experiences, and she said she "surreptitiously stole along." One day, when I thought the coast was clear, I was surreptitiously examining the contents of the tool-chest with a view toward securing to myself such hammers, saws, and what else I might need in doing some carpentry work I had planned. The tool-chest is kept in the granary; both it and the granary are usually kept locked. Now the "gude mon" has an idea that a "wooman" needs no tools, and the use and misuse of his tools have led to numbers of inter-household wars. I was gloating over my opportunity, and also making the best of it, when a medley of burring Scotch voices brought me to a quick realization that discretion is the better part of valor. So I went into seclusion behind a tall oat-bin. It seemed that two neighbors whom I had never seen were preparing to go to town, and had come to get some tools and to see if the Stewart would lend them each a team. Now Mr. Stewart must be very righteous, because he certainly regardeth his beast, although he does n't always love his neighbor as himself. He was willing, however, for friends Tam Campbell and Archie McEttrick to use his teams, but he himself would take a lighter rig and go along, so as to see that his horses were properly cared for, and to help out in case of need.

They made their plans, set the day, and went their ways. As soon as I could, I made myself scarce about the granary and very busy about the house, and, like Josiah Allen, I was in a very "happyfied" state of mind. There is nothing Mr. Stewart likes better than to catch me unprepared for something.

A CONTENTED COUPLE

I had been wanting to go to town, and he had said I might go with him next time he went, if I was ready when he was. I knew I would not hear one word about the proposed trip, but that only added to the fun. I had plenty of time to make all preparations; so the day before they were to start found me with all in readiness. It was quite early in the spring and the evenings were quite chilly. We had just finished supper, when we heard a great rumbling, and I knew neighbors Campbell and McEttrick had arrived on their way to town; so I began to prepare supper for them. I had n't expected a woman, and was surprised when I saw the largest, most ungainly person I have ever met come shambling toward me.

She was Aggie McEttrick. She is tall and raw-boned, she walks with her toes turned out, she has a most peculiar lurching gait like a camel's. She has skin the color of a new saddle, and the oddest straggly straw-colored hair. She never wears corsets and never makes her waists long enough, so there is always a streak of gray undershirt visible about her waist. Her skirts are never long enough either, and she knits her own stockings. Those inclined can always get a good glimpse of blue-and-white striped hose. She said, "I guess you are the Missus." And that was every word she said until I had supper on the table. The men were busy with their teams, and she sat with her feet in my oven, eyeing my every movement. I told her we had just had our supper, but she waited until I had theirs ready before she announced that neither she nor Archie ate hot biscuits or steak, that they did n't take tea for supper, preferred coffee, and that neither of them could eat peaches or honey. So all of my supper was ruled off except the butter and cream. She went down to their wagons and brought up what she wanted, so Tam Campbell was the only one who ate my honey and biscuit.

Tam is just a Scot with an amazingly close

fist, and he is very absent-minded. I had met Annie, his wife, and their six children. She told me of his absent-mindedness. Her remedy for his trouble when it came to household needs was to repeat the article two or three times in the list. People out like we are buy a year's supply at a time. So a list of needed things is made up and sent into town. Tam always managed to forget a great many things.

Well, bedtime came. I offered to show them to their room, but Aggie said, "We'll nae sleep in your bed. We'll jest bide in the kitchen." I could not persuade her to change her mind. Tam slept at the barn in order to see after the "beasties," should they need attention during the night. As I was preparing for bed, Aggie thrust her head into my room and announced that she would be up at three o'clock. I am not an early bird, so I thought I would let Aggie get her own breakfast, and I told her she would find everything in the pantry. As long as I was

awake I could hear Archie and Aggie talking, but I could not imagine what about. I
didn't know their habits so well as I came
to later. Next morning the rumbling of their
wagons awakened me, but I turned over and
slept until after six.

There are always so many things to do before leaving that it was nine o'clock before
we got started. We had only gotten about
two miles, when Mr. Stewart remembered
he had not locked the granary, so back we
trotted. We nooned only a few miles from
home. We knew we could not catch the
wagons before camping-time unless we drove
very hard, so Mr. Stewart said we would
go by the Edmonsons' and spend the night
there. I enjoy even the memory of that drive
through the short spring afternoon, — the
warm red sand of the desert; the Wind River
Mountains wrapped in the blue veil of distance; the sparse gray-green sage, ugly in
itself, but making complete a beautiful picture; the occasional glimpse we had of shy,

beautiful wild creatures. So much happiness can be crowded into so short a time. I was glad, though, when Cora Belle's home became a part of our beautiful picture. It is situated among great red buttes, and there is a blue lake back of the house. Around the lake is a fringe of willows. Their house is a low, rambling affair, with a long, low porch and a red clay roof. Before the house is a cotton-wood tree, its gnarled, storm-twisted branches making it seem to have the "rheumatiz." There is a hop-vine at one end of the porch. It had not come out when we were there, but the dead vine clung hopelessly to its supports.

Little Cora Belle just bubbled with delight, and her grandparents were scarcely better than she. Spring house-cleaning was just finished, and they have company so seldom that they made us feel that we were doing them a favor by stopping. Poor old "Pa" hobbled out to help put the team away, and when they came back, Cora Belle asked me

out to help prepare supper, so I left Mr.
Stewart with "Granny" and "Pa" to listen
to their recitals and to taste their many
medicines. Cora Belle is really an excellent
housekeeper. Her cooking would surprise
many people. Her bread was delicious, and I
am sure I never tasted anything better than
the roasted leg of lamb she gave us for supper.
I am ashamed to tell you how much I ate of
her carrot jam. From where I sat I had a
splendid view of the sunset across the lake.
Speaking of things singly, Wyoming has
nothing beautiful to offer. Taken altogether,
it is grandly beautiful, and at sunrise and
sunset the "heavens declare His glory."

Cora Belle is so animated and so straight-
forward, so entirely clean in all her thoughts
and actions, that she commands love and
respect at one and the same time. After supper her grandfather asked her to sing and
play for us. Goodness only knows where
they got the funny little old organ that Cora
Belle thinks so much of. It has spots all over

it of medicine that has been spilled at different times, and it has, as Cora Belle said, lost
its voice in spots; but that does n't set back
Cora Belle at all, she plays away just as if
it was all right. Some of the keys keep up
a mournful whining and groaning, entirely
outside of the tune. Cora Belle says they
play themselves. After several "pieces" had
been endured, "Pa" said, "Play my piece,
Cory Belle"; so we had "Bingen on the
Rhine" played and sung from A to izzard.
Dear old "Pa," his pain-twisted old face
just beamed with pride. I doubt if heaven
will have for him any sweeter music than his
"baby's" voice. Granny's squeaky, trembly
old voice trailed in after Cora Belle's, always
a word or two behind. "Tell my friends and
companions when they meet and *scrouge*
around"; that is the way they sang it, but no
one would have cared for that, if they had
noticed with what happy eagerness the two
sang together. The grandparents would like
to have sat up all night singing and telling of

things that happened in bygone days, but poor tired little Cora Belle began to nod, so we retired. As we were preparing for bed it suddenly occurred to Mr. Stewart that I had not been surprised when going to town was mentioned, so he said, "Wooman, how did it happen that you were ready when I was to gae to the toone?" "Oh," I said, "I knew you were going." "Who tell it ye?" "A little bird." "'T was some fool wooman, mayhap." I did n't feel it necessary to enlighten him, and I think he is still wondering how I knew.

Next morning we were off early, but we did n't come up with the wagons until almost camping-time. The great heavily-loaded wagons were creaking along over the heavy sands. The McEttricks were behind, Aggie's big frame swaying and lurching with every jolt of the wagon. They never travel without their German socks. They are great thick things to wear on the outside of their shoes. As we came up behind them, we could see Aggie's big socks dangling and bobbing beside Archie's from where they were tied on the back part of the wagon. We could hear them talking and see them gesticulating. When we came nearer, we found they were quarreling, and they kept at it as long as I was awake that night. After the men had disposed of their loads, they and Mr. Stewart were going out of town to where a new coalmine was being opened. I intended to go on the train to Rock Springs to do some shopping. Aggie said she was going also. I suggested that we get a room together, as we would have to wait several hours for the train, but she was suspicious of my motives. She is greatly afraid of being "done," so she told me to get my own room and pay for it. We got into town about three o'clock in the afternoon, and the train left at midnight.

I had gone to my room, and Jerrine and myself were enjoying a good rest after our fatiguing drive, when my door was thrown open and a very angry Aggie strode in. They asked us fifty cents each for our rooms. Aggie paid hers under protest and afterward got to wondering how long she was entitled to its use. She had gone back to the clerk about it, and he had told her for that night only. She argued that she should have her room for a quarter, as she would only use it until midnight. When that failed, she asked for her money back, but the clerk was out of patience and refused her that. Aggie was angry all through. She vowed she was being robbed. After she had berated me soundly for submitting so tamely, she flounced back to her own room, declaring she would get even with the robbers. I had to hurry like everything that night to get myself and Jerrine ready for the train, so I could spare no time for Aggie. She was not at the depot, and Jerrine and I had to go on to Rock Springs without her. It is only a couple of hours from Green River to Rock Springs, so I had a good nap and a late breakfast. I did my shopping and was back at Green River at two that afternoon. The first person I saw was Aggie. She sat in the depot, glowering at everybody. She had a basket of eggs and a pail of butter, which she had been trying to sell. She was waiting for the night train, the only one she could get to Rock Springs. I asked her had she overslept. "No, I didna," she replied. Then, she proceeded to tell me that, as she had paid for a whole night's use of a room, she had stayed to get its use. That it had made her plans miscarry did n't seem to count.

After all our business was attended to, we started for home. The wagons were half a day ahead of us. When we came in sight, we could see Aggie fanning the air with her long arms, and we knew they were quarreling. I remarked that I could not understand how persons who hated each other so could live together. Clyde told me I had much to learn, and said that really he knew of no other couple who were actually so devoted. He said to prove it I should ask Aggie into the buggy with me and he would get in with Archie, and afterwards we would compare notes. He drove up alongside of them, and Aggie seemed glad to make the exchange. As we had the buggy, we drove ahead of the wagons. It seems that Archie and Aggie are each jealous of the other. Archie is as ugly a little monkey as it would be possible to imagine. She bemeaned him until at last I asked her why she did n't leave him, and added that I would not stand such crankiness for one moment. Then she poured out the vials of her wrath upon my head, only I don't think they were vials but barrels.

About sundown we made it to where we intended to camp and found that Mrs. O'Shaughnessy had established a sheep-camp there, and was out with her herd herself, having only Manny, a Mexican boy she had brought up herself, for a herder. She welcomed us cordially and began supper for our entire bunch. Soon the wagons came, and all was confusion for a few minutes getting the horses put away for the night. Aggie went to her wagon as soon as it stopped and made

secure her butter and eggs against a possible
raid by Mrs. O'Shaughnessy. Having asked
too high a price for them, she had failed to
sell them and was taking them back. After
supper we were sitting around the fire, Tam
going over his account and lamenting that
because of his absent-mindedness he had
bought a whole hundred pounds of sugar
more than he had intended, Aggie and
Archie silent for once, pouting I suspect.
Clyde smiled across the camp-fire at me and
said, "Gin ye had sic a lass as I hae, ye might
blither." "Gin ye had sic a mon as mine —"
I began, but Mrs. O'Shaughnessy said, "Gin
ye had sic a mon as I hae." Then we all
three laughed, for we had each heard the
same thing, and we knew the McEttricks
would n't fight each other. They suspected
us of laughing at them, for Archie said to
Aggie, "Aggie, lass, is it sport they are making of our love?" "'T is daft they be, Archie,
lad; we'll nae mind their blither." She arose
and shambled across to Archie and hunkered

her big self down beside him. We went to
bed and left them peaceable for once.

I am really ashamed of the way I have
treated you, but I know you will forgive me.
I am not strong yet, and my eyes are still
bothering me, but I hope to be all right soon
now, and I promise you a better letter next
time. Jerrine is very proud of her necklace.
I think they are so nice for children. I can
remember how proud I was of mine when I
was a child. Please give your brother our
thanks, and tell him his little gift made my
little girl very happy.

I am afraid this letter will seem rather
jumbled. I still want the address of your
friend in Salem or any other. I shall find
time to write, and I am not going to let my
baby prevent me from having many enjoyable outings. We call our boy Henry Clyde
for his father. He is a dear little thing, but
he is a lusty yeller for baby's rights.

With much love,

JERRINE AND HER MAMMA.

XIII

October 14, 1911.

DEAR MRS. CONEY, —

I think you must be expecting an answer to your letter by now, so I will try to answer as many of your questions as I remember. Your letter has been mislaid. We have been very much rushed all this week. We had the thresher crew two days. I was busy cooking for them two days before they came, and have been busy ever since cleaning up after them. Clyde has taken the thresher on up the valley to thresh for the neighbors, and all the men have gone along, so the children and I are alone. No, I shall not lose my land, although it will be over two years before I can get a deed to it. The five years in which I am required to "prove up" will have passed by then. I could n't have held my homestead if Clyde had also been proving up, but he had accomplished that years ago and has his deed, so I am allowed my homestead. Also I have not yet used my desert right, so I am still entitled to one hundred and sixty acres more. I shall file on that much some day when I have sufficient money of my own earning. The law requires a cash payment of twenty-five cents per acre at the filing, and one dollar more per acre when final proof is made. I should not have married if Clyde had not promised I should meet all my land difficulties unaided. I wanted the fun and the experience. For that reason I want to earn every cent that goes into my own land and improvements myself. Sometimes I almost have a brain-storm wondering how I am going to do it, but I know I shall succeed; other women have succeeded. I know of several who are now where they can laugh at past trials. Do you know? — I am a firm believer in laughter. I am real superstitious about it. I think if Bad Luck came along, he would take to his heels if some one laughed right loudly.

I think Jerrine must be born for the law. She always threshes out questions that arise, to her own satisfaction, if to no one else's. She prayed for a long time for her brother; also she prayed for some puppies. The puppies came, but we did n't let her know they were here until they were able to walk. One morning she saw them following their mother, so she danced for joy. When her little brother came she was plainly disappointed. "Mamma," she said, "did God really make the baby?" "Yes, dear." "Then He has n't treated us fairly, and I should like to know why. The puppies could walk when He finished them; the calves can, too. The pigs can, and the colt, and even the chickens. What is the use of giving us a half-finished baby? He has no hair, and no teeth; he can't walk or talk, nor do anything else but squall and sleep."

After many days she got the question

settled. She began right where she left off. "I know, Mamma, why God gave us such a half-finished baby; so he could learn our ways, and no one else's, since he must live with us, and so we could learn to love him. Every time I stand beside his buggy he laughs and then I love him, but I don't love Stella nor Marvin because they laugh. So that is why." Perhaps that is the reason.

Zebbie's kinsfolk have come and taken him back to Yell County. I should not be surprised if he never returned. The Lanes and the Pattersons leave shortly for Idaho, where "our Bobbie" has made some large investments.

I hope to hear from you soon and that you are enjoying every minute. With much love,

Your friend,

ELINORE STEWART.

XIV

THE NEW HOUSE

December 1, 1911.

Dear Mrs. Coney, —

I feel just like visiting to-night, so I am going to "play like" you have come. It is so good to have you to chat with. Please be seated in this low rocker; it is a present to me from the Pattersons and I am very proud of it. I am just back from the Patterson ranch, and they have a dear little boy who came the 20th of November and they call him Robert Lane.

I am sure this room must look familiar to you, for there is so much in it that was once yours. I have two rooms, each fifteen by fifteen, but this one on the south is my "really" room and in it are my treasures. My house faces east and is built up against a side-hill, or should I say hillside? Anyway,

137

they had to excavate quite a lot. I had them
dump the dirt right before the house and
terrace it smoothly. I have sown my terrace
to California poppies, and around my porch,
which is six feet wide and thirty long, I have
planted wild cucumbers.

Every log in my house is as straight as a
pine can grow. Each room has a window and
a door on the east side, and the south room
has two windows on the south with space
between for my heater, which is one of those
with a grate front so I can see the fire burn.
It is almost as good as a fireplace. The logs
are unhewed outside because I like the rough
finish, but inside the walls are perfectly
square and smooth. The cracks in the walls
are snugly filled with "daubing" and then
the walls are covered with heavy gray
building-paper, which makes the room very
warm, and I really like the appearance. I
had two rolls of wall-paper with a bold rose
pattern. By being very careful I was able to
cut out enough of the roses, which are divided

in their choice of color as to whether they should be red, yellow, or pink, to make a border about eighteen inches from the ceiling. They brighten up the wall and the gray paper is fine to hang pictures upon. Those you have sent us make our room very attractive. The woodwork is stained a walnut brown, oil finish, and the floor is stained and oiled just like it. In the corners by the stove and before the windows we take our comfort.

From some broken bamboo fishing-rods I made frames for two screens. These I painted black with some paint that was left from the buggy, and Gavotte fixed the screens so they will stay balanced, and put in casters for me. I had a piece of blue curtain calico and with brass-headed tacks I put it on the frame of Jerrine's screen, then I mixed some paste and let her decorate it to suit herself on the side that should be next her corner. She used the cards you sent her. Some of the people have a suspiciously tottering appearance, perhaps not so very artistic, but they all mean something to a little girl whose small fingers worked patiently to attain satisfactory results. She has a set of shelves on which her treasures of china are arranged. On the floor is a rug made of two goatskins dyed black, a present from Gavotte, who heard her admiring Zebbie's bearskin. She has a tiny red rocking-chair which she has outgrown, but her rather dilapidated family of dolls use it for an automobile. For a seat for herself she has a small hassock that you gave me, and behind the blue screen is a world apart.

My screen is made just like Jerrine's except that the cover is cream material with sprays of wild roses over it. In my corner I have a cot made up like a couch. One of my pillows is covered with some checked gingham that "Dawsie" cross-stitched for me. I have a cabinet bookcase made from an old walnut bedstead that was a relic of the Mountain Meadow Massacre. Gavotte made it for me. In it I have my few books, some odds and ends of china, all gifts, and a few fossil curios. For a floor-covering I have a braided rug of blue and white, made from old sheets and Jerrine's old dresses. In the center of my room is a square table made of pine and stained brown. Over it is a table-cover that you gave me. Against the wall near my bed is my "dresser." It is a box with shelves and is covered with the same material as my screen. Above it I have a mirror, but it makes ugly faces at me every time I look into it. Upon the wall near by is a match-holder that you gave me. It is the heads of two fisher-folk. The man has lost his nose, but the old lady still thrusts out her tongue. The material on my screen and "dresser" I bought for curtains, then decided to use some white crossbar I had. But I wish I had not, for every time I look at them I think of poor little Mary Ann Parker.

I am going to make you a cup of tea and wonder if you will see anything familiar about the teapot. You should, I think, for it

A WOMAN HOMESTEADER

is another of your many gifts to me. Now I feel that you have a fairly good idea of what my house looks like, on the inside anyway. The magazines and Jerrine's cards and Mother Goose book came long ago, and Jerrine and I were both made happy. I wish I could do nice things for you, but all I can do is to love you.

Your sincere friend,

ELINORE RUPERT.

XV

THE "STOCKING-LEG" DINNER

February, 1912.

DEAR MRS. CONEY, —

. . . This time I want to tell you about a "stocking-leg" dinner which I attended not long ago. It does n't sound very respectable, but it was one of the happiest events I ever remember.

Mrs. Louderer was here visiting us, and one afternoon we were all in the kitchen when Gavotte came skimming along on the first pair of snowshoes I ever saw. We have had lots of snow this winter, and many of the hollows and gullies are packed full. Gavotte had no difficulty in coming, and he had come for the mail and to invite us to a feast of "ze hose." I could not think what kind of a dinner it could be, and I did not believe that Mr. Stewart would go, but after Gavotte had explained how much easier it was now than at any other time because the hard-packed snow made it possible to go with bobsleds, I knew he would go. I can't say I really wanted to go, but Mrs. Louderer took it for granted that it would be delightful, so she and Mr. Stewart did the planning. Next morning Gavotte met Mrs. O'Shaughnessy and invited her. Then, taking the mail, he went on ahead to blaze a trail we should follow with the sleds. We were to start two days later. They planned we could easily make the trip in a day, as, with the gulches filled with snow, short cuts were possible, and we could travel at a good pace, as we would have a strong team. To me it seemed dangerous, but dinner-parties have not been so plenty that I could miss one. So, when the day came on which we were to start, we were up betimes and had a mess-box packed and Mr. Stewart had a big pile of rocks hot. We all wore our warmest clothes, and the rest carried out hot rocks and blankets while I put the kitchen in such order that the men left to feed the stock would have no trouble in getting their meals. Mr. Stewart carried out the mess-box, and presently we were off. We had a wagon-box on bobsleds, and the box was filled with hay and hot rocks with blankets on top and more to cover us. Mr. Stewart had two big bags of grain in front, feed for the horses, and he sat on them.

It was a beautiful day and we jogged along merrily. We had lots of fun, and as we went a new way, there was much that was new to Mrs. O'Shaughnessy and myself, and it was all new to the rest. Gavotte had told us where we should noon, and we reached the place shortly after twelve. Mr. Stewart went to lift out the mess-box, — but he had forgotten to put it in! Oh, dear! We were a disappointed lot. I don't think I was ever so hungry, but there was nothing for it but to grin and bear it. It did me some good, though, to remember how a man misses his dinner. The horses had to be fed, so we walked about while they were eating. We went up a cañon that had high cliffs on one side, and came to a place where, high up on the rock wall, in great black letters, was this legend: "Dick fell off of this here clift and died." I should think there would be no question that any one who fell from that place on to the boulders below *would* die.

Soon we started again, and if not quite so jolly as we were before, at least we looked forward to our supper with a keen relish and the horses were urged faster than they otherwise would have been. The beautiful snow is rather depressing, however, when there is snow everywhere. The afternoon passed swiftly and the horses were becoming jaded. At four o'clock it was almost dark. We had been going up a deep cañon and came upon an appalling sight. There had been a snowslide and the cañon was half-filled with snow, rock, and broken trees. The whole way was blocked, and what to do we did n't know, for the horses could hardly be gotten along and we could not pass the snow-slide. We were twenty-five miles from home, night was almost upon us, and we were almost starved. But we were afraid to stay in that cañon lest more snow should slide and bury us, so sadly we turned back to find as comfortable a place as we could to spend the night. The prospects were very discouraging, and I am afraid we were all near tears, when suddenly there came upon the cold air a clear blast from a horn. Mrs. Louderer cried, "Ach, der reveille!" Once I heard a lecturer tell of climbing the Matterhorn and the calls we heard brought his story to mind. No music could have been so beautiful. It soon became apparent that we were being signaled; so we drove in the direction of the sound and found ourselves going up a wide cañon. We had passed the mouth of it shortly before we had come to the slide. Even the tired horses took new courage, and every few moments a sweet, clear call put new heart into us. Soon we saw a light. We had to drive very slowly and in places barely crept. The bugler changed his notes and we knew he was wondering if we were coming, so Mr. Stewart helloed. At once we had an answer, and after that we were steadily guided by the horn. Many times we could not see the light, but we drove in the right direction because we could hear the horn.

At last, when it was quite dark and the horses could go no farther, we drew up before the fire that had been our beacon light. It was a bonfire built out upon a point of rock at the end of the cañon. Back from it among the pines was a 'dobe house. A dried-up mummy of a man advanced from the fire to meet us, explaining that he had seen us through his field-glasses and, knowing about the snow-slide, had ventured to attract us to his poor place. Carlota Juanita was within, prepared for the *señoras*, if they would but walk in. If they would! More dead than alive, we scrambled out, cold-stiffened and hungry. Carlota Juanita threw open the low, wide door and we stumbled into comfort. She hastened to help us off with our wraps, piled more wood on the open fire, and busied herself to make us welcome and comfortable. Poor Carlota Juanita! Perhaps you think she was some slender, limpid-eyed, olive-cheeked beauty. She was fat and forty, but not fair. She had the biggest wad of hair that I ever saw, and her face was so fat that her eyes looked beady. She wore an old heelless pair of slippers or sandals that would hardly stay on, and at every step they made the most exasperating sliding noise, but she was all kindness and made us feel very welcome. The floor was of dirt, and they had the largest fireplace I have ever seen, with the widest, cleanest hearth, which was where they did their cooking. All their furniture was home-made, and on a low bench near the door were three water-jars which, I am sure, were handmade. Away back in a corner they had a small altar, on which was a little statue of Mary and the Child. Before it, suspended by a wire from the rafters, was a cow's horn in which a piece of punk was burning, just as the incense is kept burning in churches. Supper was already prepared and was simmering and smoking on the hearth. As soon as the men came in, Carlota Juanita put it on the table, which was bare of cloth. I can't say that I really like Mexican bread, but they certainly know how to cook meat. They had a most wonderful pot-roast with potatoes and corn dumplings that were delicious. The roast had been slashed in places and small bits of garlic, pepper, bacon, and, I think, parsley, inserted. After it and the potatoes and the dumplings were done, Carlota had poured in a can of tomatoes. You may not think that was good, but I can assure you it was and that we did ample justice to it. After we had eaten until we were hardly able to swallow, Carlota Juanita served a queer Mexican pie. It was made of dried buffalo-berries, stewed and made very sweet. A layer of batter had been poured into a deep baking-dish, then the berries, and then more batter. Then it was baked and served hot with plenty of hard sauce; and it was powerful good, too. She had very peculiar coffee with goat's milk in it. I took mine without the milk, but I could n't make up my mind that I liked the coffee. We sat around the fire drinking it, when Manuel Pedro Felipe told us it was some he had brought from Mexico. I did n't know they raised it there, but he told us many interesting things about it. He and Carlota Juanita both spoke fairly good English. They had lived for many years in their present home and had some sheep, a few goats, a cow or two, a few pigs, and chickens and turkeys. They had a small patch of land that Carlota Juanita tilled and on which was raised the squaw corn that hung in bunches from the rafters. Down where we live we can't get sweet corn to mature, but here, so much higher up, they have a sheltered little nook where they are able to raise many things. Upon a long shelf above the fire was an ugly old stone image, the bottom broken off and some plaster applied to make it set level. The ugly thing they had brought with them from some old ruined temple in Mexico. We were all so very tired that soon Carlota Juanita brought out an armful of the thickest, brightest rugs and spread them over the floor for us to sleep upon. The men retired to a lean-to room, where they slept, but not before Manuel Pedro Felipe and Carlota had knelt before their altar for their devotions. Mrs. O'Shaughnessy and myself and Jerrine, knowing the rosary, surprised them by kneeling with them. It is good to meet with kindred faith away off in the mountains. It seems there could not possibly be a mistake when people so far away from creeds and doctrines hold to the faith of their child-hood and find the practice a pleasure after so many years. The men bade us good-night, and we lost no time in settling ourselves to rest. Luckily we had plenty of blankets.

Away in the night I was awakened by a noise that frightened me. All was still, but instantly there flashed through my mind tales of murdered travelers, and I was almost paralyzed with fear when again I heard that stealthy, sliding noise, just like Carlota Juanita's old slippers. The fire had burned down, but just then the moon came from behind a cloud and shone through the window upon Carlota Juanita, who was asleep with her mouth open. I could also see a pine bough which was scraping against the wall outside, which was perhaps making the noise. I turned over and saw the punk burning, which cast a dim light over the serene face of the Blessed Virgin, so all fear vanished and I slept as long as they would let me in the morning. After a breakfast of *tortillas*, cheese, and rancid butter, and some more of the coffee, we started again for the stocking-leg dinner. Carlota Juanita stood in the door, waving to us as long as we could see her, and Manuel P. F. sat with Mr. Stewart to guide us around the snow-slide. Under one arm he carried the horn with which he had called us to him. It came from some long-horned cow in Mexico, was beautifully polished, and had a fancy rim of silver. I should like to own it, but I could not make it produce a sound. When we were safe on our way our guide left us, and our spirits ran high again. The horses were feeling good also, so it was a merry, laughing party that drew up before Zebbie's two hours later.

Long before I had lent Gavotte a set of the Leather-Stocking Tales, which he had read aloud to Zebbie. Together they had planned a Leather-Stocking dinner, at which should be served as many of the viands mentioned in the Tales as possible. We stayed two days and it was one long feast. We had venison served in half a dozen different ways. We had antelope; we had porcupine, or hedgehog, as Pathfinder called it; and also we had beaver-tail, which he found toothsome, but which I did *not*. We had grouse and sage hen. They broke the ice and snared a lot of trout. In their cellar they had a barrel of trout prepared exactly like mackerel, and they were more delicious than mackerel because they were finer-grained. I had been a little disappointed in Zebbie after his return from home. It seemed to me that Pauline had spoiled him. I guess I was jealous. This time he was the same little old Zebbie I had first seen. He seemed to thoroughly enjoy our visit, and I am sure we each had the time of our lives. We made it home without mishap the same day we started, all of us sure life held something new and enjoyable after all.

If nothing happens there are some more good times in store for me this summer. Gavotte once worked under Professor Marsden when he was out here getting fossils for the Smithsonian Institution, and he is very interesting to listen to. He has invited us to go with him out to the Bad-Land hills in the summer to search for fossils. The hills are only a few miles from here and I look forward to a splendid time.

XVI

THE HORSE-THIEVES

[No date.]

DEAR MRS. CONEY, —

. . . I am so afraid that you will get an overdose of culture from your visit to the Hub and am sending you an antidote of our sage, sand, and sunshine.

Mrs. Louderer had come over to see our boy. Together we had prepared supper and were waiting for Clyde, who had gone to the post-office. Soon he came, and after the usual friendly wrangling between him and Mrs. Louderer we had supper. Then they began their inevitable game of cribbage, while I sat near the fire with Baby on my lap. Clyde was telling us of a raid on a ranch about seventy-five miles away, in which the thieves had driven off thirty head of fine horses. There were only two of the thieves, and the sheriff with a large posse was pursuing them and forcing every man they came across into the chase, and a regular man-hunt was on. It was interesting only because one of the thieves was a noted outlaw then out on parole and known to be desperate. We were in no way alarmed; the trouble was all in the next county, and somehow that always seems so far away. We knew if the men ever came together there would be a pitched battle, with bloodshed and death, but there seemed little chance that the sheriff would ever overtake the men.

I remember I was feeling sorry for the poor fellows with a price on their heads, — the little pink man on my lap had softened my heart wonderfully. Jerrine was enjoying the pictures in a paper illustrating early days on the range, wild scenes of roping and branding. I had remarked that I did n't believe there were any more such times, when Mrs. Louderer replied, "Dot yust shows how much it iss you do not know. You shall come to mine house and when away you come it shall be wiser as when you left." I had kept at home very closely all summer, and a little trip seemed the most desirable thing I could think of, particularly as the baby would be in no way endangered. But long ago I learned that the quickest way to get what I want is not to want it, outwardly, at least. So I assumed an indifference that was not very real. The result was that next morning every one was in a hurry to get me started, — Clyde greasing the little old wagon that looks like a twin to Cora Belle's, and Mrs. Louderer, who thinks no baby can be properly brought up without goose-grease, busy greasing the baby "so as he shall not some cold take yet." Mrs. Louderer had ridden over, so her saddle was laid in the wagon and her pony, Bismarck, was hitched in with Chub, the laziest horse in all Wyoming. I knew Clyde could manage very well while I should be gone, and there was n't a worry to interfere with the pleasure of my outing.

A WOMAN HOMESTEADER

We jogged along right merrily, Mrs. Louderer devoting her entire attention to trying to make Chub pull even with Bismarck, Jerrine and myself enjoying the ever-changing views. I wish I could lay it all before you. Summer was departing with reluctant feet, unafraid of Winter's messengers, the chill winds. That day was especially beautiful. The gleaming snow peaks and heavy forest south and at our back; west, north, and east, long, broken lines of the distant mountains with their blue haze. Pilot Butte to the north, one hundred miles away, stood out clear and distinct as though we could drive there in an hour or two. The dull, neutral-colored "Bad Land" hills nearer us are interesting only because we know they are full of the fossil remains of strange creatures long since extinct.

For a distance our way lay up Henry's Fork valley; prosperous little ranches dotted the view, ripening grain rustled pleasantly in the warm morning sunshine, and closely cut alfalfa fields made bright spots of emerald against the dun landscape. The quaking aspens were just beginning to turn yellow; everywhere purple asters were a blaze of glory except where the rabbit-bush grew in clumps, waving its feathery plumes of gold. Over it all the sky was so deeply blue, with little, airy, white clouds drifting lazily along. Every breeze brought scents of cedar, pine, and sage. At this point the road wound along the base of cedar hills; some magpies were holding a noisy caucus among the trees, a pair of bluebirds twittered excitedly upon a fence, and high overhead a great black eagle soared. All was so peaceful that horse-thieves and desperate men seemed too remote to think about.

Presently we crossed the creek and headed our course due north toward the desert and the buttes. I saw that we were not going right to reach Mrs. Louderer's ranch, so I asked where we were supposed to be going. "We iss going to the mouth of Dry Creek by, where it goes Black's Fork into. Dere mine punchers holdts five huntert steers. We shall de camp visit and you shall come back wiser as when you went."

Well, we both came away wiser. I had thought we were going only to the Louderer ranch, so I put up no lunch, and there was nothing for the horses either. But it was too beautiful a time to let such things annoy us. Anyway, we expected to reach camp just after noon, so a little delay about dinner did n't seem so bad. We had entered the desert by noon; the warm, red sands fell away from the wheels with soft, hissing sounds. Occasionally a little horned toad sped panting along before us, suddenly darting aside to watch with bright, cunning eyes as we passed. Some one had placed a buffalo's skull beside a big bunch of sage and on the sage a splendid pair of elk's antlers. We saw many such scattered over the sands, grim reminders of a past forever gone.

About three o'clock we reached our destination, but no camp was there. We were more disappointed than I can tell you, but Mrs. Louderer merely went down to the river, a few yards away, and cut an armful of willow sticks wherewith to coax Chub to a little brisker pace, and then we took the trail of the departed mess-wagon. Shortly, we topped a low range of hills, and beyond, in a cuplike valley, was the herd of sleek beauties feeding contentedly on the lush green grass. I suppose it sounds odd to hear desert and river in the same breath, but within a few feet of the river the desert begins, where nothing grows but sage and greasewood. In oasis-like spots will be found plenty of grass where the soil is nearer the surface and where sub-irrigation keeps the roots watered. In one of these spots the herd was being held. When the grass became short they would be moved to another such place.

It required, altogether, fifteen men to take care of the herd, because many of the cattle had been bought in different places, some in

A WOMAN HOMESTEADER

Utah, and these were always trying to run away and work back toward home, so they required constant herding. Soon we caught the glimmer of white canvas, and knew it was the cover of the mess-wagon, so we headed that way.

The camp was quite near the river so as to be handy to water and to have the willows for wood. Not a soul was at camp. The fire was out, and even the ashes had blown away. The mess-box was locked and Mrs. Louderer's loud calls brought only echoes from the high rock walls across the river. However, there was nothing to do but to make the best of it, so we tethered the horses and went down to the river to relieve ourselves of the dust that seemed determined to unite with the dust that we were made of. Mrs. Louderer declared she was "so mat as nodings and would fire dot Herman so soon as she could see him already."

Presently we saw the most grotesque figure approaching camp. It was Herman, the fat cook, on Hunks, a gaunt, ugly old horse, whose days of usefulness under the saddle were past and who had degenerated into a workhorse. The disgrace of it seemed to be driving him into a decline, but he stumbled along bravely under his heavy load. A string of a dozen sage chickens swung on one side, and across the saddle in front of Herman lay a young antelope. A volley of German abuse was hurled at poor Herman, wound up in as plain American as Mrs. Louderer could speak: "And who iss going to pay de game warden de fine of dot antelope what you haf shot? And how iss it that we haf come de camp by und so starved as we iss hungry, and no cook und no food? Iss dat for why you iss paid?"

Herman was some Dutch himself, however. "How iss it," he demanded, "dat you haf not so much sense as you haf tongue? How haf you lived so long as always in de West und don't know enough to hunt a bean-hole when you reach your own camp. Hey?"

A WOMAN HOMESTEADER

Mrs. Louderer was very properly subdued and I delighted when he removed the stones from where the fire had been, exposing a pit from which, with a pair of pot-hooks, he lifted pots and ovens of the most delicious meat, beans, and potatoes. From the mess-box he brought bread and apricot pie. From a near-by spring he brought us a bright, new pail full of clear, sparkling water, but Mrs. Louderer insisted upon tea and in a short time he had it ready for us. The tarpaulin was spread on the ground for us to eat from, and soon we were showing an astonished cook just how much food two women and a child could get away with. I ate a good deal of ashes with my roast beef and we all ate more or less sand, but fastidiousness about food is a good thing to get rid of when you come West to camp.

When the regular supper-time arrived the punchers began to gather in, and the "boss," who had been to town about some business, came in and brought back the news of the

man-hunt. The punchers sat about the fire,
eating hungrily from their tin plates and
eagerly listening to the recital. Two of the
boys were tenderfeet: one from Tennessee
called "Daisy Belle," because he whistled
that tune so much and because he had
nose-bleed so much, — could n't even ride a
broncho but his nose would bleed for hours
afterwards; and the other, "N'Yawk," so
called from his native State. N'Yawk was a
great boaster; said he was n't afraid of no
durned outlaw, — said his father had waded
in bloody gore up to his neck and that he
was a chip off the old block, — rather hoped
the chase would come our way so he could
try his marksmanship.

The air began to grow chill and the sky
was becoming overcast. Preparations for the
night busied everybody. Fresh ponies were
being saddled for the night relief, the hard-
ridden, tired ones that had been used that
day being turned loose to graze. Some poles
were set up and a tarpaulin arranged for

Mrs. Louderer and me to sleep under. Mrs. Louderer and Jerrine lay down on some blankets and I unrolled some more, which I was glad to notice were clean, for Baby and myself. I can't remember ever being more tired and sleepy, but I could n't go to sleep. I could hear the boss giving orders in quick, decisive tones. I could hear the punchers discussing the raid, finally each of them telling exploits of his favorite heroes of outlawry. I could hear Herman, busy among his pots and pans. Then he mounted the tongue of the mess-wagon and called out, "We haf for breakfast cackle-berries, first vot iss come iss served, und those vot iss sleep late gets nodings."

I had never before heard of cackle-berries and asked sleepy Mrs. Louderer what they were. "Vait until morning and you shall see," was all the information that I received.

Soon a gentle, drizzling rain began, and the punchers hurriedly made their beds, as they did so twitting N'Yawk about making his between our tent and the fire. "You're dead right, pard," I heard one of them say, "to make your bed there, fer if them outlaws comes this way they'll think you air one of the women and they won't shoot you. Just us *men* air in danger."

"Confound your fool tongues, how they goin' to know there's any women here? I tell you, fellers, my old man waded in bloody gore up to his neck and I'm just like him."

They kept up this friendly parleying until I dozed off to sleep, but I could n't stay asleep. I don't think I was afraid, but I certainly was nervous. The river was making a sad, moaning sound; the rain fell gently, like tears. All nature seemed to be mourning about something, happened or going to happen. Down by the river an owl hooted dismally. Half a mile away the night-herders were riding round and round the herd. One of them was singing, — faint but distinct came his song: "Bury me not on the lone prairie." Over and over again he sang it.

After a short interval of silence he began again. This time it was, "I'm thinking of my dear old mother, ten thousand miles away."

Two punchers stirred uneasily and began talking. "Blast that Tex," I heard one of them say, "he certainly has it bad to-night. What the deuce makes him sing so much? I feel like bawling like a kid; I wish he'd shut up." "He's homesick; I guess we all are too, but they ain't no use staying awake and letting it soak in. Shake the water off the tarp, you air lettin' water catch on your side an' it's running into my ear."

That is the last I heard for a long time. I must have slept. I remember that the baby stirred and I spoke to him. It seemed to me that something struck against the guy-rope that held our tarpaulin taut, but I wasn't sure. I was in that dozy state, half asleep, when nothing is quite clear. It seemed as though I had been listening to the tramp of feet for hours and that a whole army must be filing past, when I was brought suddenly into keen consciousness by a loud voice demanding, "Hello! Whose outfit is this?" "This is the 7 Up, — Louderer's," the boss called back; "what's wanted?" "Is that you, Mat? This is Ward's posse. We been after Meeks and Murdock all night. It's so durned dark we can't see, but we got to keep going; their horses are about played. We changed at Hadley's, but we ain't had a bite to eat and we got to search your camp." "Sure thing," the boss answered, "roll off and take a look. Hi, there, you Herm, get out of there and fix these fellers something to eat."

We were surrounded. I could hear the clanking of spurs and the sound of the wet, tired horses shaking themselves and rattling the saddles on every side. "Who's in the wickiup?" I heard the sheriff ask. "Some women and kids, — Mrs. Louderer and a friend."

In an incredibly short time Herman had a

fire coaxed into a blaze and Mat Watson and the sheriff went from bed to bed with a lantern. They searched the mess-wagon, even, although Herman had been sleeping there. The sheriff unceremoniously flung out the wood and kindling the cook had stored there. He threw back the flap of our tent and flashed the lantern about. He could see plainly enough that there were but the four of us, but I wondered how they saw outside where the rain made it worse, the lantern was so dirty. "Yes," I heard the sheriff say, "we 've been pushing them hard. They 're headed north, evidently intend to hit the railroad but they 'll never make it. Every ford on the river is guarded except right along here, and there 's five parties ranging on the other side. My party 's split, — a bunch has gone on to the bridge. If they find anything they 're to fire a volley. Same with us. I knew they could n't cross the river nowhere but at the bridge or here."

The men had gathered about the fire and

were gulping hot coffee and cold beef and bread. The rain ran off their slickers in little rivulets. I was sorry the fire was not better, because some of the men had on only ordinary coats, and the drizzling rain seemed determined that the fire should not blaze high.

Before they had finished eating we heard a shot, followed by a regular medley of dull booms. The men were in their saddles and gone in less time than it takes to tell it. The firing had ceased save for a few sharp reports from the revolvers, like a coyote's spiteful snapping. The pounding of the horse's hoofs grew fainter, and soon all was still. I kept my ears strained for the slightest sound. The cook and the boss, the only men up, hurried back to bed. Watson had risen so hurriedly that he had not been careful about his "tarp" and water had run into his bed. But that would n't disconcert anybody but a tenderfoot. I kept waiting in tense silence to hear them come back with dead or wounded, but there was not a sound. The rain had stopped. Mrs. Louderer struck a match and said it was three o'clock. Soon she was asleep. Through a rift in the clouds a star peeped out. I could smell the wet sage and the sand. A little breeze came by, bringing Tex's song once more: —

"Oh, it matters not, so I've been told,
    How the body lies when the heart grows cold."

Oh, dear! the world seemed so full of sadness. I kissed my baby's little downy head and went to sleep.

It seems that cowboys are rather sleepyheaded in the morning and it is a part of the cook's job to get them up. The next I knew, Herman had a tin pan on which he was beating a vigorous tattoo, all the time hollering, "We haf cackle-berries und antelope steak for breakfast." The baby was startled by the noise, so I attended to him and then dressed myself for breakfast. I went down to the little spring to wash my face. The morning was lowering and gray, but a wind had

THE HORSE-THIEVES

sprung up and the clouds were parting. There are times when anticipation is a great deal better than realization. Never having seen a cackle-berry, my imagination pictured them as some very luscious wild fruit, and I was so afraid none would be left that I could n't wait until the men should eat and be gone. So I surprised them by joining the very earliest about the fire. Herman began serving breakfast. I held out my tin plate and received some of the steak, an egg, and two delicious biscuits. We had our coffee in big enameled cups, without sugar or cream, but it was piping hot and *so* good. I had finished my egg and steak and so I told Herman I was ready for my cackle-berries.

"Listen to her now, will you?" he asked. And then indignantly, "How many cackle-berries does you want? You haf had so many as I haf cooked for you." "Why, Herman, I have n't had a single berry," I said. Then such a roar of laughter. Herman gazed at me in astonishment, and Mr. Watson gently explained to me that eggs and cackle-berries were one and the same.

N'Yawk was not yet up, so Herman walked over to his bed, kicked him a few times, and told him he would scald him if he did n't turn out. It was quite light by then. N'Yawk joined us in a few minutes. "What the deuce was you fellers kicking up such a rumpus fer last night?" he asked. "You blamed blockhead, don't you know?" the boss answered. "Why, the sheriff searched this camp last night. They had a battle down at the bridge afterwards and either they are all killed or else no one is hurt. They would have been here otherwise. Ward took a shot at them once yesterday, but I guess he did n't hit; the men got away, anyway. And durn your sleepy head! you just lay there and snored. Well, I'll be danged!" Words failed him, his wonder and disgust were so great.

N'Yawk turned to get his breakfast. His light shirt was blood-stained in the back, —

seemed to be soaked. "What's the matter with your shirt, it's soaked with blood?" some one asked. "Then that durned Daisy Belle has been crawling in with me, that's all," he said. "Blame his bleeding snoot. I'll punch it and give it something to bleed for."

Then Mr. Watson said, "Daisy ain't been in all night. He took Jesse's place when he went to town after supper." That started an inquiry and search which speedily showed that some one with a bleeding wound had gotten in with N'Yawk. It also developed that Mr. Watson's splendid horse and saddle were gone, the rope that the horse had been picketed with lying just as it had been cut from his neck.

Now all was bustle and excitement. It was plainly evident that one of the outlaws had lain hidden on N'Yawk's bed while the sheriff was there, and that afterwards he had saddled the horse and made his escape. His own horse was found in the willows, the saddle cut loose and the bridle off, but the poor, jaded thing had never moved. By sunup the search-party returned, all too worn-out with twenty-four hours in the saddle to continue the hunt. They were even too worn-out to eat, but flung themselves down for a few hours' rest. The chase was hopeless anyway, for the search-party had gone north in the night. The wounded outlaw had doubtless heard the sheriff talking and, the coast being clear to the southward, had got the fresh horse and was by that time probably safe in the heavy forests and mountains of Utah. His getting in with N'Yawk had been a daring ruse, but a successful one. Where his partner was, no one could guess. But by that time all the camp excepting Herman and Mrs. Louderer were so panicky that we could n't have made a rational suggestion.

N'Yawk, white around his mouth, approached Mrs. Louderer. "I want to quit," he said. "Well," she said, calmly sipping her coffee, "you haf done it." "I'm sick," he stammered. "I know you iss," she said, "I haf before now seen men get sick when they iss scared to death." "My old daddy —" he began. "Yes, I know, he waded the creek vone time und you has had cold feet effer since."

Poor fellow, I felt sorry for him. I had cold feet myself just then, and I was powerfully anxious to warm them by my own fire where a pair of calm blue eyes would reassure me.

I did n't get to see the branding that was to have taken place on the range that day. The boss insisted on taking the trail of his valued horse. He was very angry. He thought there was a traitor among the posse. Who started the firing at the bridge no one knew, and Watson said openly that it was done to get the sheriff away from camp.

My own home looked mighty good to me when we drove up that evening. I don't want any more wild life on the range, — not for a while, anyway.

Your ex-Washlady,
ELINORE RUPERT STEWART.

XVII

AT GAVOTTE'S CAMP

MY DEAR FRIEND, —

At last I can write you as I want to. I am afraid you think I am going to wait until the "bairns" are grown up before writing to my friends, but indeed I shall not. I fully intend to "gather roses while I may." Since God has given me two blessings, children and friends, I shall enjoy them both as I go along.

I must tell you why I have not written as I should have done. All summer long my eyes were so strained and painful that I had to let all reading and writing go. And I have suffered terribly with my back. But now I am able to be about again, do most of my own work, and my eyes are much better. So now I shall not treat you so badly again. If you could only know how kind every one is to me, you would know that even ill health has its compensations out here. Dear Mrs. Louderer, with her goose-grease, her bread, and her delicious "kuchens." Mrs. O'Shaughnessy, with her cheery ways, her tireless friendship, and willing, capable hands. Gavotte even, with his tidbits of game and fish. Dear little Cora Belle came often to see me, sometimes bringing me a little of Grandpa's latest cure, which I received on faith, for, of course, I could not really swallow any of it. Zebbie's nephew, Parker Carter, came out, spent the summer with him, and they have now gone back to Yell County, leaving Gavotte in charge again.

Gavotte had a most interesting and prosperous summer. He was commissioned by a wealthy Easterner to procure some fossils. I had had such a confined summer that Clyde took me out to Gavotte's camp as soon as I was able to sit up and be driven. We found him away over in the bad lands camped in a fine little grove. He is a charming man to visit at any time, and we found him in a particularly happy mood. He had just begun to quarry a gigantic find; he had piles of specimens; he had packed and shipped some rare specimens of fossil plants, but his "beeg find" came later and he was jubilant. To dig fossils successfully requires great care and knowledge, but it is a work in which Gavotte excels. He is a splendid cook. I almost believe he could make a Johnny Reb like codfish, and that night we had a delicious supper and all the time listening to a learned discourse about prehistoric things. I enjoyed the meal and I enjoyed the talk, but I could not sleep peacefully for being chased in my dreams by pterodactyls, dinosaurs, and iguanodons, besides a great many horrible creatures whose names I have forgotten. Of course, when the ground begins to freeze and snow comes, fossil-mining is done for until summer comes, so Gavotte tends the critters and traps this winter. I shall not get to go to the mountains this winter. The babies are too small, but there is always some happy and interesting thing happening, and I shall have two pleasures each time, my own enjoyment, and getting to tell you of them.

XVIII

THE HOMESTEADER'S MARRIAGE AND A LITTLE FUNERAL

December 2, 1912.

DEAR MRS. CONEY, —

Every time I get a new letter from you I get a new inspiration, and I am always glad to hear from you.

I have often wished I might tell you all about my Clyde, but have not because of two things. One is I could not even begin without telling you what a good man he is, and I did n't want you to think I could do nothing but brag. The other reason is the haste I married in. I am ashamed of that. I am afraid you will think me a Becky Sharp of a person. But although I married in haste, I have no cause to repent. That is very fortunate because I have never had one bit of leisure to repent in. So I am lucky all around. The engagement was powerfully short because both agreed that the trend of events and ranch work seemed to require that we be married first and do our "sparking" afterward. You see, we had to chink in the wedding between times, that is, between planting the oats and other work that must be done early or not at all. In Wyoming ranchers can scarcely take time even to be married in the springtime. That having been settled, the license was sent for by mail, and as soon as it came Mr. Stewart saddled Chub and went down to the house of Mr. Pearson, the justice of the peace and a friend of long standing. I had never met any of the family and naturally rather dreaded to have them come, but Mr. Stewart was firm in wanting to be married at home, so he told Mr. Pearson he wanted him and his family to come up the following Wednesday and serve papers on the "wooman i' the hoose." They were astonished, of course, but being such good friends they promised

him all the assistance they could render.
They are quite the dearest, most interesting
family! I have since learned to love them
as my own.

Well, there was no time to make wedding
clothes, so I had to "do up" what I did have.
Is n't it queer how sometimes, do what you
can, work will keep getting in the way until
you can't get anything done? That is how
it was with me those few days before the
wedding; so much so that when Wednesday
dawned everything was topsy-turvy and I
had a very strong desire to run away. But
I always did hate a "piker," so I stood pat.
Well, I had most of the dinner cooked, but it
kept me hustling to get the house into anything like decent order before the old dog
barked, and I knew my moments of liberty
were limited. It was blowing a perfect hur-
ricane and snowing like midwinter. I had
bought a beautiful pair of shoes to wear on
that day, but my vanity had squeezed my
feet a little, so while I was so busy at work I

had kept on a worn old pair, intending to put on the new ones later; but when the Pearsons drove up all I thought about was getting them into the house where there was fire, so I forgot all about the old shoes and the apron I wore.

I had only been here six weeks then, and was a stranger. That is why I had no one to help me and was so confused and hurried. As soon as the newcomers were warm, Mr. Stewart told me I had better come over by him and stand up. It was a large room I had to cross, and how I did it before all those strange eyes I never knew. All I can remember very distinctly is hearing Mr. Stewart saying, "I will," and myself chiming in that I would, too. Happening to glance down, I saw that I had forgotten to take off my apron or my old shoes, but just then Mr. Pearson pronounced us man and wife, and as I had dinner to serve right away I had no time to worry over my odd toilet. Anyway the shoes were comfortable and the apron white, so I suppose it could have been worse; and I don't think it has ever made any difference with the Pearsons, for I number them all among my most esteemed friends.

It is customary here for newlyweds to give a dance and supper at the hall, but as I was a stranger I preferred not to, and so it was a long time before I became acquainted with all my neighbors. I had not thought I should ever marry again. Jerrine was always such a dear little pal, and I wanted to just knock about foot-loose and free to see life as a gypsy sees it. I had planned to see the Cliff-Dwellers' home; to live right there until I caught the spirit of the surroundings enough to live over their lives in imagination anyway. I had planned to see the old missions and to go to Alaska; to hunt in Canada. I even dreamed of Honolulu. Life stretched out before me one long, happy jaunt. I aimed to see all the world I could, but to travel unknown bypaths to do it. But first I wanted to try homesteading.

THE HOMESTEADER'S MARRIAGE

But for my having the grippe, I should never have come to Wyoming. Mrs. Seroise, who was a nurse at the institution for nurses in Denver while I was housekeeper there, had worked one summer at Saratoga, Wyoming. It was she who told me of the pine forests. I had never seen a pine until I came to Colorado; so the idea of a home among the pines fascinated me. At that time I was hoping to pass the Civil-Service examination, with no very definite idea as to what I would do, but just to be improving my time and opportunity. I never went to a public school a day in my life. In my childhood days there was no such thing in the Indian Territory part of Oklahoma where we lived, so I have had to try hard to keep learning. Before the time came for the examination I was so discouraged because of the grippe that nothing but the mountains, the pines, and the clean, fresh air seemed worth while; so it all came about just as I have written you.

So you see I was very deceitful. Do you

remember, I wrote you of a little baby boy
dying? That was my own little Jamie, our
first little son. For a long time my heart was
crushed. He was such a sweet, beautiful boy.
I wanted him so much. He died of erysipelas.
I held him in my arms till the last agony was
over. Then I dressed the beautiful little
body for the grave. Clyde is a carpenter; so
I wanted him to make the little coffin. He
did it every bit, and I lined and padded it,
trimmed and covered it. Not that we could
n't afford to buy one or that our neighbors
were not all that was kind and willing; but
because it was a sad pleasure to do everything for our little first-born ourselves.

As there had been no physician to help, so
there was no minister to comfort, and I could
not bear to let our baby leave the world
without leaving any message to a community
that sadly needed it. His little message to us
had been love, so I selected a chapter from
John and we had a funeral service, at which
all our neighbors for thirty miles around

THE HOMESTEADER'S MARRIAGE

were present. So you see, our union is sealed by love and welded by a great sorrow.

Little Jamie was the first little Stewart. God has given me two more precious little sons. The old sorrow is not so keen now. I can bear to tell you about it, but I never could before. When you think of me, you must think of me as one who is truly happy. It is true, I want a great many things I have n't got, but I don't want them enough to be discontented and not enjoy the many blessings that are mine. I have my home among the blue mountains, my healthy, well-formed children, my clean, honest husband, my kind, gentle milk cows, my garden which I make myself. I have loads and loads of flowers which I tend myself. There are lots of chickens, turkeys, and pigs which are my own special care. I have some slow old gentle horses and an old wagon. I can load up the kiddies and go where I please any time. I have the best, kindest neighbors and I have my dear absent friends. Do you wonder I am so happy? When I think of it all, I wonder how I can crowd all my joy into one short life. I don't want you to think for one moment that you are bothering me when I write you. It is a real pleasure to do so. You're always so good to let me tell you everything. I am only afraid of trying your patience too far. Even in this long letter I can't tell you all I want to; so I shall write you again soon. Jerrine will write too. Just now she has very sore fingers. She has been picking gooseberries, and they have been pretty severe on her brown little paws.

With much love to you, I am

"Honest and truly" yours,

ELINORE RUPERT STEWART.

XIX

THE ADVENTURE OF THE CHRISTMAS TREE

January 6, 1913.

My dear Friend, —

I have put off writing you and thanking you for your thought for us until now so that I could tell you of our very happy Christmas and our deer hunt all at once.

To begin with, Mr. Stewart and Junior have gone to Boulder to spend the winter. Clyde wanted his mother to have a chance to enjoy our boy, so, as he had to go, he took Junior with him. Then those of my dear neighbors nearest my heart decided to prevent a lonely Christmas for me, so on December 21st came Mrs. Louderer, laden with an immense plum pudding and a big *"wurst,"* and a little later came Mrs. O'Shaughnessy on her frisky pony, Chief, her scarlet sweater making a bright bit of color against our snow-wrapped horizon. Her face and ways are just as bright and cheery as can be. When she saw Mrs. Louderer's pudding and sausage she said she had brought nothing because she had come to get something to eat herself, "and," she continued, "it is a private opinion of mine that my neighbors are so glad to see me that they are glad to feed me." Now would n't that little speech have made her welcome anywhere?

Well, we were hilariously planning what Mrs. O'Shaughnessy called a "widdy" Christmas and getting supper, when a great stamping-off of snow proclaimed a newcomer. It was Gavotte, and we were powerfully glad to see him because the hired man was going to a dance and we knew Gavotte would contrive some unusual amusement. He had heard that Clyde was going to have a deer-drive, and did n't know that he had gone, so he had come down to join the hunt just for the fun, and was very much disappointed to find there was going to be no hunt.

CHRISTMAS TREE ADVENTURE

After supper, however, his good humor returned and he told us story after story of big hunts he had had in Canada. He worked up his own enthusiasm as well as ours, and at last proposed that we have a drive of our own for a Christmas "joy." He said he would take a station and do the shooting if one of us would do the driving. So right now I reckon I had better tell you how it is done.

There are many little parks in the mountains where the deer can feed, although now most places are so deep in snow that they can't walk in it. For that reason they have trails to water and to the different feeding-grounds, and they can't get through the snow except along these paths. You see how easy it would be for a man hidden on the trail to get one of the beautiful creatures if some one coming from another direction startled them so that they came along that particular path.

So they made their plans. Mrs. O'Shaughnessy elected herself driver. Two miles away is a huge mountain called Phillipeco, and deer were said to be plentiful up there. At one time there had been a sawmill on the mountain, and there were a number of deserted cabins in which we could make ourselves comfortable. So it was planned that we go up the next morning, stay all night, have the hunt the following morning, and then come home with our game.

Well, we were all astir early the next morning and soon grain, bedding, and chuckbox were in the wagon. Then Mrs. Louderer, the *kinder*, and myself piled in; Mrs. O'Shaughnessy bestrode Chief, Gavotte stalked on ahead to pick our way, and we were off.

It was a long, tedious climb, and I wished over and over that I had stayed at home; but it was altogether on Baby's account. I was so afraid that he would suffer, but he kept warm as toast. The day was beautiful, and the views many times repaid us for any hardship we had suffered. It was three o'clock before we reached the old mill camp.

CHRISTMAS TREE ADVENTURE

Soon we had a roaring fire, and Gavotte made the horses comfortable in one of the cabins. They were bedded in soft, dry sawdust, and were quite as well off as if they had been in their own stalls. Then some rough planks were laid on blocks, and we had our first meal since breakfast. We called it supper, and we had potatoes roasted in the embers, Mrs. Louderer's *wurst*, which she had been calmly carrying around on her arm like a hoop and which was delicious with the bread that Gavotte toasted on long sticks; we had steaming coffee, and we were all happy; even Baby clapped his hands and crowed at the unusual sight of an open fire. After supper Gavotte took a little stroll and returned with a couple of grouse for our breakfast. After dark we sat around the fire eating peanuts and listening to Gavotte and Mrs. Louderer telling stories of their different great forests. But soon Gavotte took his big sleeping-bag and retired to another cabin, warning us that we must be up early.

A WOMAN HOMESTEADER

Our improvised beds were the most comfortable things; I love the flicker of an open fire, the smell of the pines, the pure, sweet air, and I went to sleep thinking how blest I was to be able to enjoy the things I love most.

It seemed only a short time until some one knocked on our door and we were all wide awake in a minute. The fire had burned down and only a soft, indistinct glow from the embers lighted the room, while through a hole in the roof I could see a star glimmering frostily. It was Gavotte at the door and he called through a crack saying he had been hearing queer noises for an hour and he was going to investigate. He had called us so that we need not be alarmed should we hear the noise and not find him. We scrambled into our clothes quickly and ran outdoors to listen.

I can never describe to you the weird beauty of a moonlight night among the pines when the snow is sparkling and gleaming, the deep silence unbroken even by the snapping of a twig. We stood shivering and straining our ears and were about to go back to bed when we heard faintly a long-drawn wail as if all the suffering and sorrow on earth were bound up in that one sound. We could n't tell which way it came from; it seemed to vibrate through the air and chill our hearts. I had heard that panthers cried that way, but Gavotte said it was not a panther. He said the engine and saws had been moved from where we were to another spring across the cañon a mile away, where timber for sawing was more plentiful, but he supposed every one had left the mill when the water froze so they could n't saw. He added that some one must have remained and was, perhaps, in need of help, and if we were not afraid he would leave us and go see what was wrong.

We went in, made up the fire, and sat in silence, wondering what we should see or hear next. Once or twice that agonized cry came shivering through the cold moonlight.

A WOMAN HOMESTEADER

After an age, we heard Gavotte crunching through the snow, whistling cheerily to re-assure us. He had crossed the cañon to the new mill camp, where he had found two women, loggers' wives, and some children. One of the women, he said, was "so veı᾿ seek," 't was she who was wailing so, and it was the kind of "seek" where we could be of every help and comfort.

Mrs. Louderer stayed and took care of the children while Mrs. O'Shaughnessy and I followed after Gavotte, panting and stum-bling, through the snow. Gavotte said he suspected they were short of "needfuls," so he had filled his pockets with coffee and sugar, took in a bottle some of the milk I brought for Baby, and his own flask of whis-key, without which he never travels.

At last, after what seemed to me hours of scrambling through the snow, through deep-est gloom where pines were thickest, and out again into patches of white moonlight, we reached the ugly clearing where the new camp stood. Gavotte escorted us to the door and then returned to our camp. Entering, we saw the poor, little soon-to-be mother huddled on her poor bed, while an older woman stood near warning her that the oil would soon be all gone and they would be in darkness. She told us that the sick one had been in pain all the day before and much of the night, and that she herself was worn completely out. So Mrs. O'Shaughnessy sent her to bed and we took charge.

Secretly, I felt it all to be a big nuisance to be dragged out from my warm, comfortable bed to traipse through the snow at that time of the night. But the moment poor little Molly spoke I was glad I was living, because she was a poor little Southern girl whose husband is a Mormon. He had been sent on a mission to Alabama, and the poor girl had fallen in love with his handsome face and knew nothing of Mormonism, so she had run away with him. She thought it would be so grand to live in the glorious West with so

splendid a man as she believed her husband
to be. But now she believed she was going
to die and she was glad of it because she
could not return to her "folks," and she said
she knew her husband was dead because he
and the other woman's husband, both of
whom had intended to stay there all winter
and cut logs, had gone two weeks before to
get their summer's wages and buy supplies.
Neither man had come back and there was
not a horse or any other way to get out of the
mountains to hunt them, so they believed
the men to be frozen somewhere on the road.
Rather a dismal prospect, was n't it? Molly
was just longing for some little familiar
thing, so I was glad I have not yet gotten rid
of my Southern way of talking. No West-
erner can ever understand a Southerner's
need of sympathy, and, however kind their
hearts, they are unable to give it. Only a
Southerner can understand how dear are our
peculiar words and phrases, and poor little
Molly took new courage when she found I

knew what she meant when she said she was just "honin'" after a friendly voice.

Well, soon we had the water hot and had filled some bottles and placed them around our patient, and after a couple of hours the tiny little stranger came into the world. It had been necessary to have a great fire in order to have light, so as soon as we got Baby dressed I opened the door a little to cool the room and Molly saw the morning star twinkling merrily. "Oh," she said, "that is what I will call my little girlie,— Star, dear little Star."

It is strange, is n't it? how our spirits will revive after some great ordeal. Molly had been sure she was going to die and saw nothing to live for; now that she had had a cup of hot milk and held her red little baby close, she was just as happy and hopeful as if she had never left her best friends and home to follow the uncertain fortunes of young Will Crosby. So she and I talked of ash-hoppers, smoke-houses, cotton-patches, goobers, poke-greens, and shoats, until she fell asleep.

Soon day was abroad, and so we went outdoors for a fresh breath. The other woman came out just then to ask after Molly. She invited us into her cabin, and, oh, the little Mormons were everywhere; poor, half-clad little things! Some sour-dough biscuit and a can of condensed milk was everything they had to eat. The mother explained to us that their "men" had gone to get things for them, but had not come back, so she guessed they had got drunk and were likely in jail. She told it in a very unconcerned manner. Poor thing! Years of such experience had taught her that blessed are they who expect nothing, for they shall not be disappointed. She said that if Molly had not been sick she would have walked down out of the mountains and got help.

Just then two shots rang out in quick succession, and soon Gavotte came staggering along with a deer across his shoulders. That he left for the family. From our camp he had brought some bacon and butter for Molly, and, poor though it may seem, it was a treat for her. Leaving the woman to dress the venison with her oldest boy's aid, we put out across the cañon for our own breakfast. Beside our much-beaten trail hung the second venison, and when we reached our camp and had our own delicious breakfast of grouse, bread, butter, and coffee, Gavotte took Chub and went for our venison. In a short time we were rolling homeward. Of course it did n't take us nearly so long to get home because it was downhill and the road was clearly marked, so in a couple of hours we were home.

Gavotte knew the two loggers were in Green River and were then at work storing ice for the railroad, but he had not known that their wives were left as they were. The men actually had got drunk, lost their money, and were then trying to replace it. After we debated a bit we decided we could not enjoy Christmas with those people in want up there in the cold. Then we got busy. It is sixty miles to town, although our nearest point to the railroad is but forty, so you see it was impossible to get to town to get anything. You should have seen us! Every old garment that had ever been left by men who have worked here was hauled out, and Mrs. O'Shaughnessy's deft fingers soon had a pile of garments cut. We kept the machine humming until far into the night, as long as we could keep our eyes open.

All next day we sewed as hard as we could, and Gavotte cooked as hard as he could. We had intended to have a tree for Jerrine, so we had a box of candles and a box of Christmas snow. Gavotte asked for all the bright paper we could find. We had lots of it, and I think you would be surprised at the possibilities of a little waste paper. He made gorgeous birds, butterflies, and flowers out of paper that once wrapped parcels. Then he asked us for some silk thread, but I had none, so he told us to comb our hair and give him the combings. We did, and with a drop of mucilage he would fasten a hair to a bird's back and then hold it up by the hair. At a few feet's distance it looked exactly as though the bird was flying. I was glad I had a big stone jar full of *fondant*, because we had a lot of fun shaping and coloring candies. We offered a prize for the best representation of a "nigger," and we had two dozen chocolate-covered things that might have been anything from a monkey to a mouse. Mrs. Louderer cut up her big plum pudding and put it into a dozen small bags. These Gavotte carefully covered with green paper. Then we tore up the holly wreath that Aunt Mary sent me, and put a sprig in the top of each green bag of pudding. I never had so much fun in my life as I had preparing for that Christmas.

At ten o'clock, the morning of the 24th, we were again on our way up the mountain-side. We took shovels so we could clear a road if need be. We had dinner at the old camp, and then Gavotte hunted us a way out to the new, and we smuggled our things into Molly's cabin so the children should have a real surprise. Poor, hopeless little things! Theirs was, indeed, a dull outlook.

Gavotte busied himself in preparing one of the empty cabins for us and in making the horses comfortable. He cut some pine boughs to do that with, and so they paid no attention when he cut a small tree. In the mean time we had cleared everything from Molly's cabin but her bed; we wanted her to see the fun. The children were sent to the spring to water the horses and they were all allowed to ride, so that took them out of the way while Gavotte nailed the tree into a box he had filled with dirt to hold it steady.

There were four women of us, and Gavotte, so it was only the work of a few moments to get the tree ready, and it was the most beautiful one I ever saw. Your largest bell, dear Mrs. Coney, dangled from the topmost branch. Gavotte had attached a long, stout wire to your Santa Claus, so he was able to make him dance frantically without seeming to do so. The hairs that held the birds and butterflies could not be seen, and the effect was beautiful. We had a bucket of apples rubbed bright, and these we fastened to the tree just as they grew on their own branches. The puddings looked pretty, too, and we had done up the parcels that held the clothes as attractively as we could. We saved the candy and the peanuts to put in their little stockings.

As soon as it was dark we lighted the candles and then their mother called the children. Oh, if you could have seen them! It was the very first Christmas tree they had ever seen and they did n't know what to do. The very first present Gavotte handed out was a pair of trousers for eight-years-old Brig, but he just stood and stared at the tree until his brother next in size, with an eye to the main chance, got behind him and pushed him forward, all the time exclaiming, "Go

209

on, can't you! They ain't doin' nothin' to you, they's just doin' somethin' for you." Still Brig would not put out his hand. He just shook his tousled sandy head and said he wanted a bird. So the fun kept up for an hour. Santa had for Molly a package of oatmeal, a pound of butter, a Mason jar of cream, and a dozen eggs, so that she could have suitable food to eat until something could be done.

After the presents had all been distributed we put the phonograph on a box and had a dandy concert. We played "There were Shepherds," "Ave Maria," and "Sweet Christmas Bells." Only we older people cared for those, so then we had "Arrah Wanna," "Silver Bells," "Rainbow," "Red Wing," and such songs. How delighted they were! Our concert lasted two hours, and by that time the little fellows were so sleepy that the excitement no longer affected them and they were put to bed, but they hung up their stockings first, and even Molly hung hers up too. We filled them with peanuts and candy, putting the lion's share of "niggers" into Molly's stocking.

Next morning the happiness broke out in new spots. The children were all clean and warm, though I am afraid I can't brag on the fit of all the clothes. But the pride of the wearers did away with the necessity of a fit. The mother was radiantly thankful for a warm petticoat; that it was made of a blanket too small for a bed did n't bother her, and the stripes were around the bottom anyway. Molly openly rejoiced in her new gown, and that it was made of ugly gray outing flannel she did n't know nor care. Baby Star Crosby looked perfectly sweet in her little new clothes, and her little gown had blue sleeves and they thought a white skirt only added to its beauty. And so it was about everything. We all got so much out of so little. I will never again allow even the smallest thing to go to waste. We were every one just as happy as we could be, almost as delighted as Molly was over her "niggers," and there was very little given that had not been thrown away or was not just odds and ends.

There was never anything more true than that it is more blessed to give than to receive. We certainly had a delicious dinner too, and we let Molly have all she wanted that we dared allow her to eat. The roast venison was so good that we were tempted to let her taste it, but we thought better of that. As soon as dinner was over we packed our belongings and betook ourselves homeward.

It was just dusk when we reached home. Away off on a bare hill a wolf barked. A big owl hooted lonesomely among the pines, and soon a pack of yelping coyotes went scampering across the frozen waste.

It was not the Christmas I had in mind when I sent the card, but it was a *dandy* one, just the same.

With best wishes for you for a happy, *happy* New Year,

Sincerely your friend,

ELINORE RUPERT STEWART.

XX

THE JOYS OF HOMESTEADING

January 23, 1913.

DEAR MRS. CONEY, —

I am afraid all my friends think I am very forgetful and that you think I am ungrateful as well, but I am going to plead not guilty. Right after Christmas Mr. Stewart came down with *la grippe* and was so miserable that it kept me busy trying to relieve him. Out here where we can get no physician we have to dope ourselves, so that I had to be housekeeper, nurse, doctor, and general overseer. That explains my long silence.

And now I want to thank you for your kind thought in prolonging our Christmas. The magazines were much appreciated. They relieved some weary night-watches, and the box did Jerrine more good than the medicine I was having to give her for *la grippe*. She was content to stay in bed and enjoy the contents of her box.

When I read of the hard times among the Denver poor, I feel like urging them every one to get out and file on land. I am very enthusiastic about women homesteading. It really requires less strength and labor to raise plenty to satisfy a large family than it does to go out to wash, with the added satisfaction of knowing that their job will not be lost to them if they care to keep it. Even if improving the place does go slowly, it is that much done to stay done. Whatever is raised is the homesteader's own, and there is no house-rent to pay. This year Jerrine cut and dropped enough potatoes to raise a ton of fine potatoes. She wanted to try, so we let her, and you will remember that she is but six years old. We had a man to break the ground and cover the potatoes for her and the man irrigated them once. That was all that was done until digging time, when they were ploughed out and Jerrine picked them

THE JOYS OF HOMESTEADING

up. Any woman strong enough to go out by
the day could have done every bit of the
work and put in two or three times that
much, and it would have been so much more
pleasant than to work so hard in the city
and then be on starvation rations in the
winter.

To me, homesteading is the solution of all
poverty's problems, but I realize that tem-
perament has much to do with success in
any undertaking, and persons afraid of coyotes and work and loneliness had better
let ranching alone. At the same time, any
woman who can stand her own company,
can see the beauty of the sunset, loves growing things, and is willing to put in as much
time at careful labor as she does over the
washtub, will certainly succeed; will have
independence, plenty to eat all the time, and
a home of her own in the end.

Experimenting need cost the homesteader
no more than the work, because by applying
to the Department of Agriculture at Wash-

ington he can get enough of any seed and as many kinds as he wants to make a thorough trial, and it does n't even cost postage. Also one can always get bulletins from there and from the Experiment Station of one's own State concerning any problem or as many problems as may come up. I would not, for anything, allow Mr. Stewart to do anything toward improving my place, for I want the fun and the experience myself. And I want to be able to speak from experience when I tell others what they can do. Theories are very beautiful, but facts are what must be had, and what I intend to give some time.

Here I am boring you to death with things that cannot interest you! You'd think I wanted you to homestead, would n't you? But I am only thinking of the troops of tired, worried women, sometimes even cold and hungry, scared to death of losing their places to work, who could have plenty to eat, who could have good fires by gathering the wood, and comfortable homes of their own, if they but had the courage and determination to get them.

I must stop right now before you get so tired you will not answer. With much love to you from Jerrine and myself, I am

      Yours affectionately,

            ELINORE RUPERT STEWART.

XXI

February 26, 1913.

DEAR MRS. CONEY, —

I think you will excuse my mama for not writing to thank you for black Beauty when I tell you why. I wanted to thank you myself, and I wanted to hear it read first so I could very trully thank. Mama always said horses do not talk, but now she knows they do since she read the Dear little book. I have known it along time. My own pony told me the story is very true. Many times I have see men treat horses very badly, but our Clyde dont, and wont let a workman stay if He hurts stock. I am very glad.

Mr Edding came past one day with a load of hay. he had too much load to pull up hill and there was much ice and snow but he think he can make them go up so he fighted

and sweared but they could not get up.
Mama tried to lend him some horse to help
but he was angry and was termined to make
his own pull it but at last he had to take off
some hay I wish he may read my Black
Beauty.

Our Clyde is still away. We were going to
visit Stella. Mama was driving, the horses
raned away. We goed very fast as the wind.
I almost fall out Mama hanged on to the
lines. if she let go we may all be kill. At last
she raned them into a fence. they stop and a
man ran to help so we are well but mama
hands and arms are still so sore she cant
write you yet. My brother Calvin is very
sweet. God had to give him to us because he
squealed so much he sturbed the angels. We
are not angels so he Dont sturb us. I thank
you for my good little book. and I love you
for it too.

very speakfully,

JERRINE RUPERT.

XXII

THE EFFICIENT MRS. O'SHAUGHNESSY

May 5, 1913.

DEAR MRS. CONEY, —

Your letter of April 25 certainly was a surprise, but a very welcome one. We are so rushed with spring work that we don't even go to the office for the mail, and I owe you letters and thanks. I keep promising myself the pleasure of writing you and keep putting it off until I can have more leisure, but that time never gets here. I am so glad when I can bring a little of this big, clean, beautiful outdoors into your apartment for you to enjoy, and I can think of nothing that would give me more happiness than to bring the West and its people to others who could not otherwise enjoy them. If I could only take them from whatever is worrying them and give them this bracing mountain air, glimpses

EFFICIENT MRS. O'SHAUGHNESSY

of the scenery, a smell of the pines and the sage, — if I could only make them feel the free, ready sympathy and hospitality of these frontier people, I am sure their worries would diminish and my happiness would be complete.

Little Star Crosby is growing to be the sweetest little kid. Her mother tells me that she is going "back yan" when she gets a "little mo' richer." I am afraid you give me too much credit for being of help to poor little Molly. It was n't that I am so helpful, but that "fools rush in where angels fear to tread." It was Mrs. O'Shaughnessy who was the real help. She is a woman of great courage and decision and of splendid sense and judgment. A few days ago a man she had working for her got his finger-nail mashed off and neglected to care for it. Mrs. O'Shaughnessy examined it and found that gangrene had set in. She did n't tell him, but made various preparations and then told him she had heard that if there was danger of blood-poisoning it would show if the finger was placed on wood and the patient looked toward the sun. She said the person who looked at the finger could then see if there was any poison. So the man placed his finger on the chopping-block and before he could bat his eye she had chopped off the black, swollen finger. It was so sudden and unexpected that there seemed to be no pain. Then Mrs. O'Shaughnessy showed him the green streak already starting up his arm. The man seemed dazed and she was afraid of shock, so she gave him a dose of morphine and whiskey. Then with a quick stroke of a razor she laid open the green streak and immersed the whole arm in a strong solution of bichloride of mercury for twenty minutes. She then dressed the wound with absorbent cotton saturated with olive oil and carbolic acid, bundled her patient into a buggy, and drove forty-five miles that night to get him to a doctor. The doctor told us that only her quick action and knowledge of what to do saved the man's life.

EFFICIENT MRS. O'SHAUGHNESSY

I was surprised that you have had a letter from Jerrine. I knew she was writing to you that day, but I was feeling very stiff and sore from the runaway and had lain down. She kept asking me how to spell words until I told her I was too tired and wanted to sleep. While I was asleep the man came for the mail, so she sent her letter. I have your address on the back of the writing-pad, so she knew she had it right, but I suspect that was all she had right. She has written you many letters but I have never allowed her to send them because she misspells, but that time she stole a march on me. The books you sent her, "Black Beauty" and "Alice in Wonderland," have given her more pleasure than anything she has ever had. She just loves them and is saving them, she says, for her own little girls. She is very confident that the stork will one day visit her and leave her a "very many" little girls. They are to be of assorted sizes. She says she can't see why I order all my babies little and red and squally,

A WOMAN HOMESTEADER

— says she thinks God had just as soon let me have larger ones, especially as I get so many from him.

One day before long I will get busy and write you of a visit I shall make to a Mormon bishop's household. Polygamy is still practiced.

Very truly your friend,
ELINORE RUPERT STEWART.

XXIII

HOW IT HAPPENED

June 12, 1913.

DEAR MRS. CONEY, —

Your letter of the 8th to hand, and in order to catch you before you leave I'll answer at once and not wait for time. I always think I shall do better with more time, but with three "bairns," garden, chickens, cows, and housework I don't seem to find much time for anything. Now for the first question. My maiden name was Pruitt, so when I am putting on airs I sign Elinore Pruitt Stewart. I don't think I have ever written anything that Clyde would object to, so he can still stay on the pedestal Scotch custom puts him upon and remain "the Stewart." Indeed, I don't think you are too inquisitive, and I am glad to tell you how I happened to meet the "gude mon."

A WOMAN HOMESTEADER

It all happened because I had a stitch in my side. When I was housekeeper at the Nursery, I also had to attend to the furnace, and, strange but true, the furnace was built across the large basement from where the coal was thrown in, so I had to tote the coal over, and my *modus operandi* was to fill a tub with coal and then drag it across to the hungry furnace. Well, one day I felt the catch and got no better fast. After Dr. F—— punched and prodded, she said, "Why, you have the grippe." Rev. Father Corrigan had been preparing me to take the Civil-Service examination, and that afternoon a lesson was due, so I went over to let him see how little I knew. I was in pain and was so blue that I could hardly speak without weeping, so I told the Reverend Father how tired I was of the rattle and bang, of the glare and the soot, the smells and the hurry. I told him what I longed for was the sweet, free open, and that I would like to homestead. That was Saturday evening. He advised me to go straight uptown and put an "ad" in the paper, so as to get it into the Sunday paper. I did so, and because I wanted as much rest and quiet as possible I took Jerrine and went uptown and got a nice quiet room.

On the following Wednesday I received a letter from Clyde, who was in Boulder visiting his mother. He was leaving for Wyoming the following Saturday and wanted an interview, if his proposition suited me. I was so glad of his offer, but at the same time I could n't know what kind of person he was; so, to lessen any risk, I asked him to come to the Sunshine Mission, where Miss Ryan was going to help me "size him up." He did n't know that part of it, of course, but he stood inspection admirably. I was under the impression he had a son, but he had n't, and he and his mother were the very last of their race. I am as proud and happy to-day as I was the day I became his wife. I wish you knew him, but I suspect I had better not brag too much, lest you think me not quite sincere. He expected to visit you while he was in Boulder. He went to the Stock Show, but was with a party, so he planned to go again. But before he could, the man he left here, and whom I dismissed for drunkenness, went to Boulder and told him I was alone, so the foolish thing hurried home to keep me from too hard work. So that is why he was disappointed.

Junior can talk quite well, and even Calvin jabbers. The children are all well, and Jerrine writes a little every day to you. I have been preparing a set of indoor outings for invalids. Your telling me your invalid friends enjoyed the letters suggested the idea. I thought to write of little outings I take might amuse them, but wanted to write just as I took the little trips, while the impressions were fresh; that is why I have not sent them before now. Is it too late? Shall I send them to you? Now this is really not a letter; it is just a reply. I must say good-night; it is twelve o'clock, and I am so sleepy.

HOW IT HAPPENED

I do hope you will have a very happy summer, and that you will share your happiness with me in occasional letters.

With much love,

ELINORE STEWART.

In writing I forgot to say that the Reverend Father thought it a good plan to get a position as housekeeper for some rancher who would advise me about land and water rights. By keeping house, he pointed out, I could have a home and a living and at the same time see what kind of a homestead I could get.

XXIV

A LITTLE ROMANCE

October 8, 1913.

MY DEAR FRIEND, —

I have had such a happy little peep into another's romance that I think I should be cheating you if I did n't tell you. Help in this country is extremely hard to get; so when I received a letter from one Aurelia Timmons, saying she wanted a job, — three dollars a week and *not* to be called "Relie," — my joy could hardly be described. I could hardly wait until morning to start for Bridger Bench, where Aurelia held forth. I was up before the lark next morning. It is more miles to the Bridger Bench country than the "gude mon" wants his horses driven in a day; so permission was only given after I promised to curb my impatience and stay overnight with Mrs. Louderer. Under ordi-

A LITTLE ROMANCE

nary circumstances that would have been a pleasure, but I knew at least a dozen women who would any of them seize on to Aurelia and wrest her from me, so it was only after it seemed I would not get to go at all that I promised.

At length the wagon was greased, some oats put in, a substantial lunch and the kiddies loaded in, and I started on my way. Perhaps it was the prospect of getting help that gilded everything with a new beauty. The great mountains were so majestic, and the day so young that I knew the night wind was still murmuring among the pines far up on the mountain-sides. The larks were trying to outdo each other and the robins were so saucy that I could almost have flicked them with the willow I was using as a whip. The rabbit-bush made golden patches everywhere, while purple asters and great pink thistles lent their charm. Going in that direction, our way lay between a mountain stream and the foothills. There are many ranches along the stream, and as we were out so early, we could see the blue smoke curling from each house we passed. We knew that venison steak, hot biscuit, and odorous coffee would soon grace their tables. We had not had the venison, for the "gude mon" holds to the letter of the law which protects deer here, but we begrudged no one anything; we were having exactly what we wanted. We jogged along happily, if slowly, for I must explain to you that Chub is quite the laziest horse in the State, and Bill, his partner, is so old he stands like a bulldog. He is splay-footed and sway-backed, but he is a beloved member of our family, so I vented my spite on Chub, and the willow descended periodically across his black back, I guess as much from force of habit as anything else. But his hide is thick and his memory short, so we broke no record that day.

We drove on through the fresh beauty of the morning, and when the sun was straight overhead we came to the last good water we could expect before we reached Mrs. Louderer's; so we stopped for lunch. In Wyoming quantity has a great deal more to do with satisfaction than does quality; after half a day's drive you won't care so much what it is you're going to eat as you will that there is enough of it. That is a lesson I learned long ago; so our picnic was real. There were no ants in the pie, but that is accounted for by there being no pie. Our road had crossed the creek, and we were resting in the shade of a quaking-asp grove, high up on the sides of the Bad Land hills. For miles far below lay the valley through which we had come.

Farther on, the mountains with their dense forests were all wrapped in the blue haze of the melancholy days. Soon we quitted our enchanted grove whose quivering, golden leaves kept whispering secrets to us.

About three o'clock we came down out of the hills on to the bench on which the Louderer ranch is situated. Perhaps I should explain that this country is a series of huge terraces, each terrace called a bench. I had just turned into the lane that leads to the house when a horseman came cantering toward me. "Hello!" he saluted, as he drew up beside the wagon. "Goin' up to the house? Better not. Mrs. Louderer is not at home, and there's no one there but Greasy Pete. He's on a tear; been drunk two days, I'm tellin' you. He's *full* of mischief. 'T ain't safe around old Greasy. I advise you to go some- 'eres else." "Well," I asked, "where *can* I go?" "Danged if I know," he replied, "'les- sen it's to Kate Higbee's. She lives about six or seven miles west. She ain't been here long, but I guess you can't miss her place. Just jog along due west till you get to Red Gulch ravine, then turn north for a couple of miles. You'll see her cabin up against a cedar ridge. Well, so 'long!" He dug his spurs into his cayuse's side and rode on.

Tears of vexation so blinded me that I could scarcely see to turn the team, but omi- nous sounds and wild yells kept coming from the house, so I made what haste I could to get away from such an unpleasant neighborhood. Soon my spirits began to rise. Kate Higbee, I reflected, was likely to prove to be an interesting person. All Westerners are likable, with the possible exception of Greasy Pete. I rather looked forward to my visit. But my guide had failed to mention the buttes; so, although I jogged as west as I knew how, I found I had to wind around a butte about ever so often. I crossed a ravine with equal frequency, and all looked alike. It is not surprising that soon I could not guess where I was. We could turn back and retrace our tracks, but actual danger lay there; so it seemed wiser to push on, as there was, perhaps, no greater danger than discomfort ahead. The sun hung like a big red ball ready to drop into the hazy distance when we came clear of the buttes and down on to a broad plateau, on which grass grew plentifully. That encouraged me because the horses need not suffer, and if I could make the scanty remnant of our lunch do for the children's supper and breakfast, we could camp in comfort, for we had blankets. But we must find water. I stood up in the wagon and, shading my eyes against the sun's level light, was looking out in the most promising directions when I noticed that the plateau's farther side was bounded by a cedar ridge, and, better yet, a smoke was slowly rising, column-like, against the dun prospect. That, I reasoned, must be my destination. Even the horses livened their paces, and in a little while we were there.

But no house greeted our eyes, — just a big camp-fire. A lean old man sat on a log-end and surveyed us indifferently. On the ground lay a large canvas-covered pack, apparently unopened. An old saddle lay up against a cedar-trunk. Two old horses grazed near. I was powerfully disappointed. You know misery loves company; so I ventured to say, "Good-evening." He did n't stir, but he grunted, "Hello." I knew then that he was not a fossil, and hope began to stir in my heart. Soon he asked, "Are you goin' somewheres or jist travelin'?" I told him I had started somewhere, but reckoned I must be traveling, as I had not gotten there. Then he said, "My name is Hiram K. Hull. Whose woman are you?" I confessed to belonging to the house of Stewart. "Which Stewart?" he persisted, — "C. R., S. W., or H. C.?" Again I owned up truthfully. "Well," he continued, "what does he mean by letting you gad about in such onconsequential style?"

Sometimes a woman gets too angry to talk. Don't you believe that? No? Well, they do, I assure you, for I was then. He seemed grown to the log. As he had made no move to help me, without answering him I clambered out of the wagon and began to take the horses loose. "Ho!" he said; "are you goin' to camp here?" "Yes, I am," I snapped. "Have you any objections?" "Oh, no, none that won't keep," he assured me. It has always been a theory of mine that when we become sorry for ourselves we make our misfortunes harder to bear, because we lose courage and can't think without bias; so I cast about me for something to be glad about, and the comfort that at least we were safer with a simpleton than near a drunken Mexican came to me; so I began to view the situation with a little more tolerance.

After attending to the horses I began to make the children comfortable. My unwilling host sat silently on his log, drawing long and hard at his stubby old pipe. How very little there was left of our lunch! Just for meanness I asked him to share with us, and, if you'll believe me, he did. He gravely ate bread-rims and scraps of meat until there was not one bit left for even the baby's breakfast. Then he drew the back of his hand across his mouth and remarked, "I should think when you go off on a ja'nt like this you'd have a well-filled mess-box." Again speech failed me.

A LITTLE ROMANCE

Among some dwarf willows not far away a spring bubbled. I took the kiddies there to prepare them for rest. When I returned to the fire, what a transformation! The pack was unrolled and blankets were spread, the fire had been drawn aside, disclosing a bean-hole, out of which Hiram K. was lifting an oven. He took off the lid. Two of the plumpest, brownest ducks that ever tempted any one were fairly swimming in gravy. Two loaves of what he called punk, with a box of crackers, lay on a newspaper. He mimicked me exactly when he asked me to take supper with him, and I tried hard to imitate him in promptitude when I accepted. The babies had some of the crackers wet with hot water and a little of the gravy. We soon had the rest looking scarce. The big white stars were beginning to twinkle before we were through, but the camp-fire was bright, and we all felt better-natured. Men are not alone in having a way to their heart through their stomach.

I made our bed beneath the wagon, and

A WOMAN HOMESTEADER

Hiram K. fixed his canvas around, so we should be sheltered. I felt so much better and thought so much better of him that I could laugh and chat gayly. "Now, tell me," he asked, as he fastened the canvas to a wheel, "didn't you think I was an old devil at first?" "Yes, I did," I answered. "Well," he said, "I am; so you guessed right." After I put the children to bed, we sat by the fire and talked awhile. I told him how I happened to be gadding about in "such onconsequential" style, and he told me stories of when the country was new and fit to live in. "Why," he said, in a burst of enthusiasm, "time was once when you went to bed you were not sure whether you'd get up alive and with your scalp on or not, the Injins were that thick. And then there was white men a durned sight worse; they were likely to plug you full of lead just to see you kick. But now," he continued mournfully, "a bear or an antelope, maybe an elk, is about all the excitement we can expect. Them good old days are gone." I am mighty glad of it; a drunken Pete is bad enough for me.

I was tired, so soon I went to bed. I could hear him as he cut cedar boughs for his own fireside bed, and as he rattled around among his pots and pans. Did you ever eat pork and beans heated in a frying-pan on a camp-fire for breakfast? Then if you have not, there is one delight left you. But you must be away out in Wyoming, with the morning sun just gilding the distant peaks, and your pork and beans must be out of a can, heated in a disreputable old frying-pan, served with coffee *boiled* in a battered old pail and drunk from a tomato-can. You'll *never* want iced melons, powdered sugar, and fruit, or sixty-nine varieties of breakfast food, if once you sit Trilbywise on Wyoming sand and eat the kind of breakfast we had that day.

After breakfast Hiram K. Hull hitched our horses to the wagon, got his own horses ready, and then said, "'T ain't more 'n half a mile straight out between them two hills to

the stage-road, but I guess I had better go
and show you exactly, or you will be millin'
around here all day, tryin' to find it." In a
very few minutes we were on the road, and
our odd host turned to go. "S'long!" he
called. "Tell Stewart you seen old Hikum.
Him and me's shared tarps many's the
nights. We used to be punchers together,
—old Clyde and me. Tell him old Hikum
ain't forgot him." So saying, he rode away
into the golden morning, and we drove on-
ward, too.

We stopped for lunch only a few minutes
that day, and we reached the Bridger community about two that afternoon. The much
sought Aurelia had accepted the position of
lifetime housekeeper for a sheep-herder who
had no house to keep, so I had to cast about
for whatever comfort I could. The roadhouse
is presided over by a very able body of the
clan of Ferguson. I had never met her, but
formalities count for very little in the West.
She was in her kitchen, having more trouble,

A LITTLE ROMANCE

she said, than a hen whose ducklings were in swimming. I asked her if she could accommodate the children and myself. "Yes," she said, "I can give you a bed and grub, but I ain't got no time to ask you nothing. I ain't got no time to inquire who you are nor where you come from. There's one room left. You can have that, but you'll have to look out for yourself and young 'uns." I felt equal to that; so I went out to have the horses cared for and to unload the kiddies.

Leaning against the wagon was a man who made annual rounds of all the homes in our community each summer; his sole object was to see what kind of flowers we succeeded with. Every woman in our neighborhood knows Bishey Bennet, but I don't think many would have recognized him that afternoon. I had never seen him dressed in anything but blue denim overalls and overshirt to match, but to-day he proudly displayed what he said was his dove-colored suit. The style must have been one of years ago, for I

cannot remember seeing trousers quite so
skimpy. He wore top-boots, but as a con-
cession to fashion he wore the boot-tops under the trouser-legs, and as the trousers were
about as narrow as a sheath skirt, they kept
slipping up and gave the appearance of being at least six inches too short. Although
Bishey is tall and thin, his coat was two sizes
too small, his shirt was of soft tan material,
and he wore a blue tie. But whatever may
have been amiss with his costume was easily
forgotten when one saw his radiant face. He
grasped my hand and wrung it as if it was a
chicken's neck.

"What in the world is the matter with
you?" I asked, as I rubbed my abused paw.
"Just you come here and I'll tell you," he
answered. There was no one to hear but the
kiddies, but I went around the corner of the
house with him. He put his hand up to his
mouth and whispered that "Miss Em'ly"
was coming, would be there on the afternoon
stage. I had never heard of "Miss Em'ly,"

and said so. "Well, just you go in and set on the sofy and soon's I see your horses took care of I'll come in and tell you." I went into my own room, and after I rustled some water I made myself and the kiddies a little more presentable. Then we went into the sitting-room and sat on the "sofy." Presently Bishey sauntered in, trying to look unconcerned and at ease, but he was so fidgety he could n't sit down. But he told his story, and a dear one it is.

It seems that back in New York State he and Miss Em'ly were "young uns" together. When they were older they planned to marry, but neither wanted to settle down to the humdrumness that they had always known. Both dreamed of the golden West; so Bishey had gone to blaze the trail, and "Miss Em'ly" was to follow. First one duty and then another had held her, until twenty-five years had slipped by and they had not seen each other, but now she was coming, that very day. They would be married that evening, and I at once appointed myself matron of honor and was plumb glad there was no other candidate.

I at once took the decorations in hand. Bishey, Jerrine, and myself went out and gathered armfuls of asters and goldenrod-like rabbit-brush. From the dump-pile we sorted cans and pails that would hold water, and we made the sitting-room a perfect bower of purple and gold beauty. I put on my last clean shirt-waist and the children's last clean dresses. Then, as there seemed nothing more to do, Bishey suggested that we walk up the road and meet the stage; but the day had been warm, and I remembered my own appearance when I had come over that same road the first time. I knew that journey was trying on any one's appearance at any time of the year, and after twenty-five years to be thrust into view covered with alkali dust and with one's hat on awry would be too much for feminine patience; so I pointed out to Bishey that he 'd better clear out and let Miss

A LITTLE ROMANCE

Em'ly rest a bit before he showed up. At last he reluctantly agreed.

I went out to the kitchen to find what could be expected in the way of hot water for Miss Em'ly when she should come. I found I could have all I wanted if I heated it myself. Mrs. Ferguson could not be bothered about it, because a water company had met there to vote on new canals, the sheep-men were holding a convention, there was a more than usual run of transients besides the regular boarders, and supper was ordered for the whole push. All the help she had was a girl she just knew did n't have sense enough to pound sand into a rat-hole. Under those circumstances I was mighty glad to help. I put water on to heat and then forgot Miss Em'ly, I was enjoying helping so much, until I heard a door slam and saw the stage drive away toward the barn.

I hastened to the room I knew was reserved for Miss Em'ly. I rapped on the door, but it was only opened a tiny crack. I whispered through that I was a neighbor-friend of Mr. Bennet's, that I had lots of hot water for her and had come to help her if I might. Then she opened the door, and I entered. I found a very travel-stained little woman, down whose dust-covered cheeks tears had left their sign. Her prettiness was the kind that wins at once and keeps you ever after. She was a strange mixture of stiff reticence and childish trust. She was in *such* a flutter, and she said she was ashamed to own it, but she was so hungry she could hardly wait.

After helping her all I could, I ran out to see about the wedding supper that was to be served before the wedding. I found that no special supper had been prepared. It seemed to me a shame to thrust them down among the water company, the convention, the regulars, and the transients, and I mentally invited myself to the wedding supper and began to plan how we could have a little privacy. The carpenters were at work on a long room off the kitchen that was to be used as storeroom and pantry. They had gone for the day, and their saw-horses and benches were still in the room. It was only the work of a moment to sweep the sawdust away. There was only one window, but it was large and in the west. It took a little time to wash that, but it paid to do it. When a few asters and sprays of rabbit-brush were placed in a broken jar on the window-sill, there was a picture worth seeing. Some planks were laid on the saw-horses, some papers over them, and a clean white cloth over all. I sorted the dishes myself; the prettiest the house afforded graced our table. I rubbed the glassware until it shone almost as bright as Bishey's smile.

Bishey had come when he could stay away no longer; he and Miss Em'ly had had their first little talk, so they came out to where I was laying the table. They were both beaming. Miss Em'ly took hold at once to help. "Bishey," she commanded, "do you go at once to where my boxes are open, the one marked 7; bring me a blue jar you'll find in one corner." He went to do her bidding, and I to see about the kiddies. When I came back with them, there was a small willow basket in the center of our improvised table, heaped high with pears, apples, and grapes all a little the worse for their long journey from New York State to Wyoming, but still things of beauty and a joy as long as they lasted to Wyoming eyes and appetites. We had a perfectly roasted leg of lamb; we had mint sauce, a pyramid of flaky mashed potatoes, a big dish of new peas, a plate of sponge-cake I will be long in forgetting; and the blue jar was full of grape marmalade. Our iced tea was exactly right; the pieces of ice clinked pleasantly against our glasses. We took our time, and we were all happy. We could all see the beautiful sunset, its last rays lingering on Miss Em'ly's abundant auburn hair to make happy the bride the sun shines on. We saw the wonderful colors —

orange, rose, and violet — creep up and fade into darker shades, until at last mellow dusk filled the room. Then I took the kiddies to my room to be put to bed while I should wait until time for the ceremony.

Soon the babies were sleeping, and Jerrine and I went into the sitting-room. They were sitting on the "sofy." She was telling him that the apples had come from the tree they had played under, the pears from the tree they had set out, the grapes from the vine over the well. She told him of things packed in her boxes, everything a part of the past they both knew. He in turn told her of his struggles, his successes, and some of what he called his failures. She was a most encouraging little person, and she'd say to him, "You did well, Bishey. I'll say *that* for you: you did well!" Then he told her about the flowers he had planted for her. I understood then why he acted so queerly about my flowers. It happens that I am partial to old-time favorites, and I grow as many of them as I can get to succeed in this altitude; so I have zinnias, marigolds, hollyhocks, and many other dear old flowers that my mother loved. Many of them had been the favorites of Miss Em'ly's childhood, but Bishey had n't remembered the names; so he had visited us all, and when he found a flower he remembered, he asked the name and how we grew it, then he tried it, until at last he had about all. Miss Em'ly wiped the tears from her eyes as she remarked, "Bishey, you did well; yes, you did *real* well." I thought to myself how well we could *all* do if we were so encouraged.

At last the white-haired old justice of the peace came, and said the words that made Emily Wheeler the wife of Abisha Bennet. A powerfully noisy but truly friendly crowd wished them well. One polite fellow asked her where she was from. She told him from New York *State*. "Why," he asked, "do New Yorkers always say *State?*" "Why, because," she answered, — and her eyes were big with surprise, — "*no* one would want to say they were from New York *City*."

It had been a trying day for us, so soon Jerrine and I slipped out to our room. Ours was the first room off the sitting-room, and a long hallway led past our door; a bench sat against the wall, and it seemed a favorite roosting-place for people with long discussions. First some fellows were discussing the wedding. One thought Bishey "cracked" because he had shipped out an old cooking-stove, one of the first manufactured, all the way from where he came from, instead of buying a new one nearer home. They recalled instance after instance in which he had acted queerly, but to me his behavior was no longer a mystery. I know the stove belonged somewhere in the past and that his every act connected past and future. After they had talked themselves tired, two old fellows took possession of the bench and added a long discussion on how to grow corn to the general din. Even sweet corn cannot be successfully grown at this altitude, yet those old men argued pro and con till I know their throats must have ached. In the sitting-room they all talked at once of ditches, water-contracts, and sheep. I was *so* sleepy. I heard a tired clock away off somewhere strike two. Some sheep-men had the bench and were discussing the relative values of different dips. I reckon my ego must have gotten tangled with some one's else about then, for I found myself sitting up in bed foolishly saying, —

> "Two old herders, unshaved and hairy,
> Whose old tongues are *never* weary,
> Just outside my chamber-door
> Prate of sheep dips for *ever* more."

Next morning it was Bishey's cheerful voice that started my day. I had hoped to be up in time to see them off, but I was n't. I heard him call out to Mrs. Bishey, "Miss Em'ly, I 've got the boxes all loaded. We can start *home* in ten minutes." I heard her clear voice reply, "You 've done well, Bishey. I 'll be ready by then." I was hurriedly dressing,

A LITTLE ROMANCE

hoping yet to see her, when I heard Bishey call out to bluff old Colonel Winters, who had arrived in the night and had not known of the wedding, "Hello! Winters, have you met Miss Em'ly? Come over here and meet her. I'm a married man now. I married Miss Em'ly last night." The colonel could n't have known how apt was his reply when he said, "I'm glad for you, Bishey. You've done well." I peeked between the curtains, and saw Bishey's wagon piled high with boxes, with Miss Em'ly, self-possessed and happy, greeting the colonel. Soon I heard the rattle of wheels, and the dear old happy pair were on their way to the cabin home they had waited twenty-five years for. Bless the kind old hearts of them! I'm sure they've both "done well."

XXV

AMONG THE MORMONS

November, 1913.

My dear Friend, —

I have wanted to write you for a long time, but have been so busy. I have had some visitors and have been on a visit; I think you would like to hear about it all, so I will tell you.

I don't think you would have admired my appearance the morning this adventure began: I was in the midst of fall house-cleaning which included some papering. I am no expert at the very best, and papering a wall has difficulties peculiar to itself. I was up on a barrel trying to get a long, sloppy strip of paper to stick to the ceiling instead of to me, when in my visitors trooped, and so surprised me that I stepped off the barrel and into a candy-bucket of paste. At the same time the paper came off the ceiling and fell over mine and Mrs. Louderer's head. It was right aggravating, I can tell you, but my visitors were Mrs. O'Shaughnessy and Mrs. Louderer, and no one could stay discouraged with that pair around.

After we had scraped as much paste as we could off ourselves they explained that they had come to take me somewhere. That sounded good to me, but I could not see how I could get off. However, Mrs. Louderer said she had come to keep house and to take care of the children while I should go with Mrs. O'Shaughnessy to E——. We should have two days' travel by sled and a few hours on a train, then another journey by sled. I wanted to go powerfully, but the paste-smeared room seemed to forbid.

As Mrs. Louderer would stay with the children, Mr. Stewart thought the trip would be good for me. Mrs. O'Shaughnessy knew I wanted to visit Bishop D——, a shining light among the Latter-Day Saints, so she promised we should stay overnight at his house. That settled it; so in the cold, blue light of the early morning, Mr. Beeler, a new neighbor, had driven my friends over in Mrs. Louderer's big sled, to which was hitched a pair of her great horses and his own team. He is a widower and was going out to the road for supplies, so it seemed a splendid time to make my long-planned visit to the Bishop. Deep snow came earlier this year than usual, and the sledding and weather both promised to be good. It was with many happy anticipations that I snuggled down among the blankets and bearskins that morning.

Mr. Beeler is pleasant company, and Mrs. O'Shaughnessy is so jolly and bright, and I could leave home without a single misgiving with Mrs. Louderer in charge.

The evening sky was blazing crimson and gold, and the mountains behind us were growing purple when we entered the little settlement where the Bishop lives. We drove briskly through the scattered, straggling little village, past the store and the meeting-house, and drew up before the dwelling of the Bishop. The houses of the village were for the most part small cabins of two or three rooms, but the Bishop's was more pretentious. It was a frame building and boasted paint and shutters. A tithing-office stood near, and back of the house we could see a large granary and long stacks of hay. A bunch of cattle was destroying one stack, and Mrs. O'Shaughnessy remarked that the tallow from those cattle should be used when the olive oil gave out at their anointings, because it was the Bishop's cattle eating consecrated hay.

We knocked on the door, but got no answer. Mr. Beeler went around to the back, but no one answered, so we concluded we would have to try elsewhere for shelter. Mrs. O'Shaughnessy comforted me by remarking, "Well, there ain't a penny's worth of difference in a Mormon bishop and any other Mormon, and D—— is not the only polygamist by a long shot."

We had just turned out of the gate when a

lanky, tow-headed boy about fourteen years
of age rode up. We explained our presence
there, and the boy explained to us that the
Bishop and Aunt Debbie were away. The
next best house up the road was his "Maw's,"
he said; so, as Mr. Beeler expected to stay
with a friend of his, Mrs. O'Shaughnessy and
I determined to see if "Maw" could accommodate us for the night.

Mr. Beeler offered to help the boy get the
cattle out, but he said, "No, Paw said it
would not matter if they got into the hay,
but that he had to knock off some poles on
another part of the stockyard so that some
horses could get in to eat."

"But," I asked, "isn't that consecrated
hay? — isn't it tithing?"

"Yes," he said, "but that won't hurt a
bit, only that old John Ladd always pays his
tithe with foxtail hay and it almost ruins
Paw's horses' mouths."

I asked him if his father's stock was supposed to get the hay.

AMONG THE MORMONS

"No, I guess not," he said, "but they are always getting in accidental like."

We left him to fix the fence so the horses could get in "accidental like," and drove the short distance to "the next best house."

We were met at the door by a pleasant-faced little woman who hurried us to the fire. We told her our plight. "Why, certainly you must stay with me," she said. "I am glad the Bishop and Deb are away. They keep all the company, and I so seldom have any one come; you see Debbie has no children and can do so much better for any one stopping there than I can, but I like company, too, and I am glad of a chance to keep you. You two can have Maudie's bed. Maud is my oldest girl and she has gone to Ogden to visit, so we have plenty of room."

By now it was quite dark. She lighted a lamp and bustled about, preparing supper. We sat by the stove and, as Mrs. O'Shaughnessy said, "noticed."

Two little boys were getting in wood for

the night. They appeared to be about eight
years old; they were twins and were the
youngest of the family. Two girls, about ten
and twelve years old, were assisting our hostess; then the boy Orson, whom we met at
the gate, and Maud, the daughter who was
away, made up the family. They seemed a
happy, contented family, if one judged by
appearance alone. After supper the children
gathered around the table to prepare next
day's lessons. They were bright little folks,
but they mingled a great deal of talk with
their studies and some of what they talked
was family history.

"Mamma," said Kittie, the largest of the
little girls, "if Aunt Deb does buy a new coat
and you get her old one, then can I have
yours?"

"I don't know," her mother replied; "I
should have to make it over if you did take
it. Maybe we can have a new one."

"No, we can't have a new one, I know, for
Aunt Deb said so, but she is going to give me

her brown dress and you her gray one; she said so the day I helped her iron. We'll have those to make over."

For the first time I noticed the discontented lines on our hostess's face, and it suddenly occurred to me that we were in the house of the Bishop's second wife. Before I knew I was coming on this journey I thought of a dozen questions I wanted to ask the Bishop, but I could never ask that careworn little woman anything concerning their peculiar belief. However, I was spared the trouble, for soon the children retired and the conversation drifted around to Mormonism and polygamy; and our hostess seemed to want to talk, so I just listened, for Mrs. O'Shaughnessy rather likes to "argufy"; but she had no argument that night, only her questions started our hostess's story.

She had been married to the Bishop not long before the manifesto, and he had been married several years then to Debbie. But Debbie had no children, and all the money the Bishop had to start with had been his first wife's; so when it became necessary for him to discard a wife it was a pretty hard question for him because a little child was coming to the second wife and he had nothing to provide for her with except what his first wife's money paid for. The first wife said she would consent to him starting the second, if she filed on land and paid her back a small sum every year until it was all paid back. So he took the poor "second," after formally renouncing her, and helped her to file on the land she now lives on. He built her a small cabin, and so she started her career as a "second." I suppose the "first" thought she would be rid of the second, who had never really been welcome, although the Bishop could never have married a "second" without her consent.

"I would *never* consent," said Mrs. O'Shaughnessy.

"Oh, yes, you would if you had been raised a Mormon," said our hostess. "You see, we were all of us children of polygamous parents. We have been used to plural marriages all our lives. We believe that such experience fits us for our after-life, as we are only preparing for life beyond while here."

"Do you expect to go to heaven, and do you think the man who married you and then discarded you will go to heaven too?" asked Mrs. O'Shaughnessy.

"Of course I do," she replied.

"Then," said Mrs. O'Shaughnessy, "I am afraid if it had been mysilf I'd have been after raising a little hell here intirely."

Our hostess was not offended, and there followed a long recital of earlier-day hard times that you would scarcely believe any one could live through. It seems the first wife in such families is boss, and while they do not live in the same homes, still she can very materially affect the other's comfort.

Mrs. O'Shaughnessy asked her if she had married again.

She said, "No."

A WOMAN HOMESTEADER

"Then," said Mrs. O'Shaughnessy, "whose children are these?"

"My own," she replied.

Mrs. O'Shaughnessy was relentless. "Who is their father?" she asked.

I was right sorry for the poor little woman as she stammered, "I — I don't know."

Then she went on, "Of course I *do* know, and I don't believe you are spying to try to stir up trouble for my husband. Bishop D—— is their father, as he is still my husband, although he had to cast me off to save himself and me. I love him and I see no wrong in him. All the Gentiles have against him is he is a little too smart for them. 'T was their foolish law that made him wrong the children and me, and *not* his wishes."

"But," Mrs. O'Shaughnessy said, "it places your children in such a plight; they can't inherit, they can't even claim his name, they have no status legally."

"Oh, but the Bishop will see to that," the little woman answered.

AMONG THE MORMONS

Mrs. O'Shaughnessy asked her if she had still to work as hard as she used to.

"No, I don't believe I do," she said, "for since Mr. D—— has been Bishop, things come easier. He built this house with his own money, so Deb has nothing to do with it."

I asked her if she thought she was as happy as "second" as she would be if she was the *only* wife.

"Oh, I don't know," she said, "perhaps not. Deb and me don't always agree. She is jealous of the children and because I am younger, and I get to feeling bad when I think she is perfectly safe as a wife and has no cares. She has everything she wants, and I have to take what I can get, and my children have to wait upon her. But it will all come right somewhere, sometime," she ended cheerfully, as she wiped her eyes with her apron.

I felt so sorry for her and so ashamed to have seen into her sorrow that I was really glad next morning when I heard Mr. Beeler's cheerful voice calling, "All aboard!"

We had just finished breakfast, and few would ever guess that Mrs. D—— knew a trial; she was so cheerful and so cordial as she bade us good-bye and urged us to stop with her every time we passed through.

About noon that day we reached the railroad. The snow had delayed the train farther north, so for once we were glad to have to wait for a train, as it gave us time to get a bite to eat and to wash up a bit. It was not long, however, till we were comfortably seated in the train. I think a train ride might not be so enjoyable to most, but to us it was a delight; I even enjoyed looking at the Negro porter, although I suspect he expected to be called Mister. I found very soon after coming West that I must not say "Uncle" or "Aunty" as I used to at home.

It was not long until they called the name of the town at which we wanted to stop. Mrs. O'Shaughnessy had a few acquaintances there, but we went to a hotel. We were both tired, so as soon as we had supper we went to bed. The house we stopped at was warmer and more comfortable than the average hotel in the West, but the partitions were very thin, so when a couple of "punchers," otherwise cowboys, took the room next to ours, we could hear every word they said.

It appears that one was English and the other a tenderfoot. The tenderfoot was in love with a girl who had filed on a homestead near the ranch on which he was employed, but who was then a waitress in the hotel we were at. She had not seemed kind to the tenderfoot and he was telling his friend about it. The Englishman was trying to instruct him as to how to proceed.

"You need to be *very* circumspect, Johnny, where females are concerned, but you must n't be too danged timid either."

"I don't know what the devil to say to her; I can barely nod my head when she asks me will I take tea or coffee; and to-night she

mixed it because I nodded yes when she said,
'tea or coffee,' and it was the dangdest mess I
ever tried to get outside of."

"Well," the friend counseled, "you just
get her into a corner some'eres and say to 'er,
'Dearest 'Attie, I hoffer you my 'and hand
my 'eart.'"

"But I *can't*," wailed Johnny. "I could
never get her into a corner anyway."

"If you can't, you're not hold enough to
marry then. What the 'ell would you do with
a woman in the 'ouse if you could n't corner
'er? I tell 'e, women 'ave to 'ave a master,
and no man better tackle that job until 'e
can be sure 'e can make 'er walk the chalk-
line."

"But I don't want her to walk any line; I
just want her to speak to me."

"Dang me if I don't believe you are locoed.
Why, she's got 'e throwed hand 'og-tied now.
What d'e want to make it any worse for?"

They talked for a long time and the Englishman continued to have trouble with his

h's; but at last Johnny was encouraged to "corner 'er" next morning before they left for their ranch.

We expected to be astir early anyway, and our curiosity impelled us to see the outcome of the friend's counsel, so we were almost the first in the dining-room next morning. A rather pretty girl was busy arranging the tables, and soon a boyish-looking fellow, wearing great bat-wing chaps, came in and stood warming himself at the stove.

I knew at once it was Johnny, and I saw "'Attie" blush. The very indifference with which she treated him argued well for his cause, but of course he did n't know that. So when she passed by him and her skirt caught on his big spurs they both stooped at once to unfasten it; their heads hit together with such a bump that the ice was broken, although he seemed to think it was her skull. I am sure there ought to be a thaw after all his apologies. After breakfast Mrs. O'Shaughnessy went out to see her friend Cormac

O'Toole. He was the only person in town we could hope to get a team from with which to continue our journey. This is a hard country on horses at best, and at this time of the year particularly so; few will let their teams go out at any price, but Mrs. O'Shaughnessy had hopes, and she is so persuasive that I felt no one could resist her. There was a drummer at breakfast who kept "cussing" the country. He had tried to get a conveyance and had failed; so the cold, the snow, the people, and everything else disgusted him.

Soon Mrs. O'Shaughnessy returned, and as the drummer was trying to get out to E——, and that was our destination also, she made her way toward him, intending to invite him to ride with us. She wore over her best clothes an old coat that had once belonged to some one of her men friends. It had once been bearskin, but was now more *bare* skin, so her appearance was against her; she looked like something with the mange. So Mr. Drummer did not wait to hear what she was going to say but at once exclaimed, "No, madam, I cannot let you ride out with me. I can't get a rig myself in this beastly place." Then he turned to a man standing near and remarked, "These Western women are so bold they don't hesitate to *demand* favors."

Mrs. O'Shaughnessy's eyes fairly snapped, but she said nothing. I think she took a malicious delight in witnessing the drummer's chagrin when a few moments later our comfortable sleigh and good strong team appeared.

We were going to drive ourselves, but we had to drive to the depot for our suit-cases; but when we got there the ticket-office was not open, so the agent was probably having his beauty sleep. There was a fire in the big stove, and we joined the bunch of men in the depot. Among them we noticed a thin, consumptive-looking fellow, evidently a stranger.

Very soon some men began talking of some transaction in which a Bishop B—— was concerned. It seemed they did n't admire the Bishop very much; they kept talking of his peculiarities and transgressions, and mentioned his treatment of his wives. His "second," they said, was blind because of cataracts, and, although abundantly able, he left her in darkness. She had never seen her two last children. Some one spoke up and said, "I thought polygamy was no longer practiced." Then the man explained that they no longer contracted plural marriages, but that many kept *all* their wives and B—— still had both of his. He went on to say that although such practice is contrary to law, it was almost impossible to make a case against them, for the women would not swear against their husbands. B—— had been arrested once, but his second swore that she did n't know who her children's father was, and it cost the sheriff his office the next election.

Mrs. O'Shaughnessy spoke to an acquaintance of hers and mentioned where we were going. In a short while we got our suit-cases and we were off, but as we drove past the freight depot, the stranger we had noticed came down the steps and asked us to let him ride out with us. I really felt afraid of him, but Mrs. O'Shaughnessy thinks herself a match for any mere man, so she drew up and the man climbed in. He took the lines and we snuggled down under the robes and listened to the runners, shrill screeching over the frozen surface.

We had dinner with a new settler, and about two o'clock that afternoon we overtook a fellow who was plodding along the road. His name was B——, he said, and he pointed out to us his broad fields and herds. He had been overseeing some feeders he had, and his horse had escaped, so he was walking home, as it was only a couple of miles. He talked a great deal in that two-mile trip; too much for his own good, it developed.

For the first time since B—— climbed into our sleigh, the stranger spoke. "Can you tell me where Mrs. Belle B—— lives?" he asked.

"Why, yes," our passenger replied. "She is a member of our little flock. She is slightly

275

related to me, as you perhaps noticed the name, and I will show you to her house."

"Just how is she related to you?" the stranger asked.

"That," the man replied, "is a matter of protection. I have *given* her the protection of my name."

"Then she is your wife, is she not?" the stranger asked.

"You must be a stranger in this country," the man evaded. "What is your name?"

But the stranger did n't seem to hear, and just then we came opposite the residence of the Bishop, and the man we had picked up in the road said, "That is my home, won't you get out and warm? My wife will be glad to get acquainted with you ladies."

We declined, as it was only a short distance to the house of the man Mrs. O'Shaughnessy had come to see, so he stayed in the sleigh to show the stranger to the house of Mrs. Belle B——. I can't say much for it as a house, and I was glad I did n't have to go in. The stranger and B—— got out and entered the house, and we drove away.

Next morning, as we returned through the little village, it was all excitement. Bishop B —— had been shot the night before, just as he had left the house of Mrs. Belle B——, for what reason or by whom no one knew; and if the Bishop knew he had not told, for he either would not or could not talk.

They were going to start with him that day to the hospital, but they had no hopes of his living.

When we came to Mrs. Belle's house, Mrs. O'Shaughnessy got out of the sleigh and went into the house. I could hear her soothing voice, and I was mighty glad the poor, forlorn woman had such a comforter.

.   .   .   .

I was so *very* glad to get home. How good it all looked to me! "Poop o' Roome" has a calf, and as we drove up to the corral Clyde was trying to get it into the stall with the rest. It is "Poop's" first calf, and she is **very** proud of it, and objected to its being put away from her, so she bunted at Clyde, and as he dodged her, the calf ran between his feet and he sat down suddenly in the snow. I laughed at him, but I am powerfully glad he is no follower of old Joseph Smith.

Mrs. Louderer was enjoying herself immensely, she loves children so much. She and Clyde hired the "Tackler" — so called because he will tackle *any* kind of a job, whether he knows anything about it or not — to paper the room. He thinks he is a great judge of the fitness of things and of beauty. The paper has a stripe of roses, so Tackler reversed every other strip so that some of my roses are standing on their heads. Roses don't all grow one way, he claims, and so his method "makes 'em look more nachul like."

A little thing like wall-paper put on upside down don't bother me; but what *would* I do if I were a "second"?

Your loving friend,

ELINORE RUPERT STEWART.

XXVI

SUCCESS

DEAR MRS. CONEY, —

This is Sunday and I suppose I ought not to be writing, but I must write to you and I may not have another chance soon. Both your letters have reached me, and now that our questions are settled we can proceed to proceed.

Now, this is the letter I have been wanting to write you for a long time, but could not because until now I had not actually proven all I wanted to prove. Perhaps it will not interest you, but if you see a woman who wants to homestead and is a little afraid she will starve, you can tell her what I am telling you.

I never did like to theorize, and so this year I set out to prove that a woman could ranch if she wanted to. We like to grow potatoes on new ground, that is, newly cleared land on which no crop has been grown. Few weeds grow on new land, so it makes less work. So I selected my potato-patch, and the man ploughed it, although I could have done that if Clyde would have let me. I cut the potatoes, Jerrine helped, and we dropped them in the rows. The man covered them, and that ends the man's part. By that time the garden ground was ready, so I planted the garden. I had almost an acre in vegetables. I irrigated and I cultivated it myself.

We had all the vegetables we could possibly use, and now Jerrine and I have put in our cellar full, and this is what we have: one large bin of potatoes (more than two tons), half a ton of carrots, a large bin of beets, one of turnips, one of onions, one of parsnips, and on the other side of the cellar we have more than one hundred heads of cabbage. I have experimented and found a kind of squash that can be raised here, and that the ripe ones keep well and make good pies; also that the young tender ones make splendid pickles, quite equal to cucumbers. I was glad to stumble on to that, because pickles are hard to manufacture when you have nothing to work with. Now I have plenty. They told me when I came that I could not even raise common beans, but I tried and succeeded. And also I raised lots of green tomatoes, and, as we like them preserved, I made them all up that way. Experimenting along another line, I found that I could make catchup, as delicious as that of tomatoes, of gooseberries. I made it exactly the same as I do the tomatoes and I am delighted. Gooseberries were very fine and very plentiful this year, so I put up a great many. I milked ten cows twice a day all summer; have sold enough butter to pay for a year's supply of flour and gasoline. We use a gasoline lamp. I have raised enough chickens to completely renew my flock, and all we wanted to eat, and have some fryers to go into the winter with. I have enough turkeys for all of our birthdays and holidays.

A WOMAN HOMESTEADER

I raised a great many flowers and I worked several days in the field. In all I have told about I have had no help but Jerrine. Clyde's mother spends each summer with us, and she helped me with the cooking and the babies. Many of my neighbors did better than I did, although I know many town people would doubt my doing so much, but I did it. I have tried every kind of work this ranch affords, and I can do any of it. Of course I *am* extra strong, but those who try know that strength and knowledge come with doing. I just love to experiment, to work, and to prove out things, so that ranch life and "roughing it" just suit me.

THE END